Principles

of

Priesthood

Leadership

Principles
of
Priesthood
Leadership

Stephen D. Nadauld

DESERET
BOOK

SALT LAKE CITY, UTAH

Visit us at DeseretBook.com

First printing in hardbound 1999
First printing in paperbound 2009

Library of Congress Catalog Card Number 98-74769

ISBN-10 1-57008-622-2 (hardbound)
ISBN-13 978-1-60641-132-2(paperbound)

Printed in the United States of America
Malloy Lithographing Incorporated, Ann Arbor, MI

10   9   8   7   6   5   4   3   2

CONTENTS

INTRODUCTION

One of the significant challenges facing The Church of Jesus Christ of Latter-day Saints as it moves into the twenty-first century is that of preparing and training leaders who can be effective in moving forward the work of the Lord. Effective leadership is essential to the success of any organized group, whether it be a family, priesthood quorum, auxiliary, ward, or stake. Leadership is not the same as management. An organization can be well managed but not necessarily well led. The purpose of this book is to examine, in a Church context, important characteristics of leadership that differentiate leaders from managers and allow them to function effectively in leadership positions. The ideas and concepts are directed at priesthood leaders in the Church, but are equally applicable to sister leaders in Church auxiliaries.

I mean to lay forth a few simple principles which can be mastered by men and women of any level of education or background. These are organizational principles—they do not and cannot substitute for individual goodness or adherence to gospel principles. Priesthood leaders must be men of strong character who have learned to personally follow the teachings of the Savior. These are men who have the right to be taught by the Spirit, and those spiritual teachings will be the best source of leadership training and advice. Nevertheless, there are some principles of priesthood leadership that have broad applications and can aid those who wish to be more effective in their leadership roles. I would hope that in the process of reading, studying, and pondering these basic principles priesthood leaders will seek inspiration as to how they may be applied in their ministry.

I began thinking seriously about the ideas in this book shortly after an experience I had while visiting a stake conference during my first year of service as a General Authority in the Second Quorum of the Seventy. The stake had been organized for fifteen or twenty years and the members were good, faithful members of the Church. The stake presidency had been called a year earlier and were able men with strong testimonies.

As we sat and visited together, I asked a question that I had often found to be helpful in similar group sessions. "Brethren, what are you doing that is working well?" There was a long pause, and quizzical glances darted back and forth between the presidency members. Finally the stake president said, "Well, we are doing something that seems to be helpful."

He went on to explain that they had concluded to do one thing in that calendar year that was the second of their presidency. That one thing was to have every stake family visited by a stake presidency member sometime during that year. They had determined that if each member of the presidency visited four families every Sunday afternoon they could just about visit all 650 families in their stake in a year. They had been at their task for nearly three months and were still of the opinion that they could accomplish the goal.

After a few questions about the logistics of the effort, I paused and said: "Brethren, let me ask you this question. What is the purpose of your visit? What do you tell the people when you get into their homes?" They said they really didn't have a specific message, but thought their visits were helpful and mostly productive. We then went on to other matters.

As I later reflected on the experience, I realized that what these brethren were doing had merit, but I wondered if it was the most effective approach to priesthood leadership. I supposed that there must be a few fundamental principles and concepts that would help priesthood leaders be much more effective in their very important assignments to direct the Lord's work here on earth.

This book is the result of thinking about the question, What three or four concepts or principles in priority order would be most helpful to any priesthood leader? The answers to the question are based on my observations of hundreds of both effective and ineffective leaders, on ideas gleaned from many helpful training sessions taught by extraordinary General Authority leaders, and on my personal experiences in presiding over organizations.

The focus of the book is on concepts and ideas, on priorities and principles. I have tried to illustrate the concepts with appropriate stories and experiences. However, it is my observation that priesthood leaders are well versed in anecdotal or story leadership and would benefit greatly from a better conceptual framework from which to operate. I believe the framework developed here is applicable at all levels of Church leadership, from stake presidencies and bishoprics down through Melchizedek and Aaronic Priesthood quorums.

I would hope that after reading the book a priesthood holder could take out a single sheet of paper and in a few sentences outline the steps that could be taken to make him a more effective priesthood leader. The steps would reference principles in priority order and would serve to direct the energies and activities of the priesthood leader to those few most important matters that would dramatically improve his effectiveness. The outline would look like Figure 1.

Each of chapters 1, 2, and 3 discusses a single basic concept or principle that I consider to be fundamental to priesthood leadership. They are in priority order and are summarized along with several other useful notions in chapter 5. Chapter 4 lays out principles for Aaronic Priesthood leadership. Each chapter concludes with a checklist for priesthood leaders.

Figure 1

*What Can I Do to Become a More
Effective Priesthood Leader?*

I.

    A.

    B.

    C.

II.

    A.

    B.

III.

    A.

    B.

CHAPTER ONE

TEACHING THE PLAN
OF REDEMPTION

I recall an interesting conversation when our family came home from a missionary "farewell" sacrament meeting. As we worked together to set the table and prepare Sunday dinner, I asked our teenage sons what they thought about the meeting. They said, "Well, it was different!" I asked, "Was it different good or different bad?" "No, Dad, it was definitely different good. He'll be a great missionary leader, won't he!"

They were right. It was definitely good, and we all knew it and felt it. It was a wonderful illustration of the most important concept concerning leadership in the priesthood.

A Fundamental Responsibility of
Every Priesthood Leader

I remember being called as a young bishop and considering what I thought would be important things to do in order to be a good leader. I believed it would be important to start and end meetings on time, to conduct them with dignity, to have an agenda and follow it, to delegate to counselors and others, to follow through on assignments, to be available to ward members, to listen and be kind, and so forth. I now believe that these notions are best categorized as good management practice. These management practices are undoubtedly helpful to a leader, but in my view they do not set one apart as an effective leader.

We may view ourselves as managers, problem solvers, administrators, and so on, or we may define ourselves in terms of our activities, attending meetings, making assignments, doing home teaching, delegating, conducting, and so forth. These are the tasks that we have seen others perform, and we define ourselves and our service in the same terms. Indeed it is the fact that there are so many diverse ways to think about leadership and so many different things to do as a leader that it gives us pause. I believe that effective leadership in today's complex (some would say helter-skelter) environment demands that the leader have a sense of what is most important. The question facing most priesthood leaders, then, is, With everything I have to do in my Church position, what should I do that would be the most effective in moving the Lord's work forward?

The answer may surprise you. It did me. But as our children observed about the sacrament meeting, when you see it you know it. We can discover the principle together by reading in the Book of Mormon about an experience of Alma the Younger. In the twelfth chapter of Alma we learn that Alma and Amulek were teaching the people of Ammonihah when a man named Antionah, who was a chief ruler among the people, came forward and asked an interesting question: "What is this that thou hast said, that man should rise from the dead and be changed from this mortal to an immortal state, that the soul can never die? What does the scripture mean, which saith that God placed cherubim and a flaming sword on the east of the garden of Eden, lest our first parents should enter and partake of the fruit of the tree of life, and live forever? And thus we see that there was no possible chance that they should live forever." (Alma 12:20–21.)

If Antionah's question is taken at face value (without attributing any ulterior motive), it appears that Antionah had heard of certain words and phrases such as *first parents, tree of life, living forever,* and so on, and wished to better understand their meaning. Alma takes this approach and uses the question as a great teaching moment, for in verse 22 he says, "This is the thing which I was about to explain." His explanation leads to these words: "Now, if it had not been for the plan of redemption, which was laid from the foundation of the world, there could have been no resurrection of the dead; but there was a plan of redemption laid, which shall bring to pass the resurrection of the dead, of which has been spoken" (Alma 12:25).

It is helpful to pause here and be sure we understand the single key word in verse 25. Given the nature of Antionah's question, what is it? It is the word plan. Alma was explaining to Antionah that the concepts he (Antionah) struggled to understand could be linked together as part of a plan—a plan of redemption that could be comprehended and understood. We know the key principles of the plan— faith, repentance, baptism, the gift of the Holy Ghost, followed by priesthood ordination, temple endowment, and temple marriage. Of course there is much more, but the essentials are as stated.

Alma continues: "And after God had appointed that these things should come unto man, behold, then he saw that it was expedient that man should know concerning the things whereof he had appointed unto them" (Alma 12:28). What does Alma mean here by "these things"? Given the context of the previous verses, he clearly meant the plan of redemption. And so God determined that it was expedient for man to learn of the plan of redemption. He then did two things. First, we learn in verse 30 that "God conversed with men, and made known unto them the plan of redemption." Second, we read in verse 1 of chapter 13, "I would that ye should remember that the Lord God ordained priests, after his holy order, which was after the order of his Son, to teach these things unto the people."

So what did God do? He explained the plan and he ordained priests. Here it is helpful to go from the abstract to the concrete. We do that by asking, So who are the priests? And after a thoughtful pause, we reply in the words of the famous philosopher, Pogo—we have met the priests and they are us! Indeed the priests are ordained Melchizedek Priesthood holders of every dispensation, and today we are they. And what does verse 1 say we are to do? We are "to teach these things unto the people." We are to teach the plan of redemption (these things) to our Heavenly Father's children in this dispensation. Here we learn the fundamental responsibility of every Melchizedek Priesthood leader. It is to be a teacher of the plan of redemption. In other words, priesthood leaders may consider themselves in a variety of ways, but in Alma 13:1 we learn that the Lord God intended priesthood leaders first and foremost to be teachers of the plan of redemption.

And so what was "different good" that the boys had observed about the sacrament meeting? It was that the departing missionary was the principal speaker, not parents or siblings. He did not talk about his athletic experiences or super activities. He spoke directly and confidently about the principles of the gospel, about faith, about the Savior and His atonement, and the desire he had to teach these principles to the people where he was called to serve. It was a wonderful example of priesthood leadership.

Consequently we observe that outstanding presidency "leaders" lovingly, but firmly teach doctrine and principles in stake conferences, at leadership meetings, at ward conferences, and during temple recommend interviews. Effective bishopric "leaders" with gentleness and kindness teach doctrine in sacrament meetings, in Aaronic Priesthood and Young Women classes, in semi-annual interviews, and at tithing settlement. Dynamic quorum "leaders" make sure that they lead in the teaching of principles to their quorum members. The single most distinguishing feature of priesthood leadership is that the leader "leads out" as a teacher of the plan of redemption. Teaching the plan of redemption should be the number one priority on the list of things to do. It differentiates a leader from a manager, will have the greatest impact on lives, and will be the most effective of all leadership activities.

There are, from my perspective, some really interesting ideas that further support and illustrate this gospel leadership principle. If you like ideas and concepts, then read on. If you don't care about parsley on your mashed potatoes (or as one of the little boys said, "Mom, why are you putting grass on the potatoes?)" then go to page 20 and read about implications for priesthood leaders.

A Priesthood Leader's Spiritual Heritage

Return to Alma chapter 13 and look closely at how the priests come to be chosen to teach the plan. Verse 3 explains it very clearly and describes a wonderful spiritual heritage for every priesthood holder. We read, "And this is the manner after which they were ordained—being called and prepared from the foundation of the world." So those who will hold the priesthood and teach the plan have been identified prior to this mortal existence! And what is the basis for that identification? Verse 3 continues, "according to the foreknowledge of God." According to the foreknowledge of God. What does that mean? The implication is clear. God had some pre-earthly knowledge of our actions and attitudes. He knew us and we knew Him. And what did He know about us? "According to the foreknowledge of God, *on account of their exceeding faith and good works.*"

Alma teaches that those who hold the priesthood were known to God for at least two distinguishing characteristics—their exceeding faith and their good works. In other words, God had a personal "foreknowledge" of their activities.

One might wonder how it was possible to demonstrate faith (or good works) in the premortal world where there was presumably no veil and no earthly distractions. What is the nature of faith when we have a firsthand knowledge of God as our Heavenly Father? The answer is that faith then was the same as faith now—faith was having or accepting assurances as to the viability of the plan of redemption. Faith was accepting the plan, receiving and accepting assurances that it would really work, and believing in Him who would play the crucial role of Savior and Redeemer. It was not a slam dunk! We had to accept assurances that Christ would do what He said He would; that He would follow the plan. Would He come to earth as an infant, be tempted, suffer the pain . . . could He really do it?

Some of us accepted the assurances offered, some did not. Those who accepted the plan and all its ramifications stood out. In fact, it is said of them by Alma that they exercised not just faith but "exceedingly great faith" (13:3). Figuratively speaking, their hands, signifying acceptance of the plan, were held high above the rest. And Alma continues in verse 4 to say, "And thus they have been called to this holy calling [priesthood holder] on account of their faith."

And what about works? What work was there to be done in the premortal setting? I believe there was the great work of explaining, of illustrating, of declaring, of teaching the plan! There was the work of witnessing that Jesus Christ would surely do that which He said He would—the work of inviting, teaching, and convincing that He would fulfill his divine mission—would come to earth and sacrifice His life. Thus those who had faith in the plan and demonstrated that faith by working to support, explain, and promote it, truly stood out—in other words, were those who became personally identified by God as leaders.

Here is a grand key to priesthood leadership. If in the premortal setting a spirit led out by demonstrating such faith and works as to become personally close to God and thereby have it said of him, "And this is the manner after which they were ordained—being called and prepared from the foundation of the world according to the foreknowledge of God" (Alma 13:3); if this is the case, what is that spirit ordained to do in this present life?

That spirit is to do exactly that which he has done heretofore—to teach the plan of redemption, to teach it by faith and to work at accomplishing its ordinances and living its principles. What an extraordinary spiritual heritage! How useful to realize that the ordained purpose of Melchizedek Priesthood leaders is to teach the plan of redemption!

What Is Meant by
"The Plan of Redemption"

We may agree that teaching the plan of redemption is fundamental to priesthood leadership, but we also need to share a somewhat uniform notion of what "the plan of redemption" means. The scriptures have referred to our Heavenly Father's plan for His children on earth by several different names. In addition to the *plan of redemption* (Jacob 6:8; Alma 12:32; 34:16), the scriptures speak of the *plan of salvation* (Moses 6:62; Jarom 1:2; Alma 42:5), the *great plan of happiness* (Alma 42:8, 16), *plan of God* (2 Nephi 9:13; Alma 34:9), *plan of mercy* (Alma 42:15), and *the gospel*

(Matt. 24:14; 2 Nephi 30:5; 3 Nephi 27:13–21; Mormon 9:8). A review of each of these terms and how they are used in the scriptures suggests that each has reference to fundamental principles and ordinances that constitute a plan for returning to our Heavenly Father's presence. Modern prophets have confirmed this concept.

It is interesting to ask priesthood leaders the question, "What are the simple steps necessary for your redemption?" The responses generally lead to a listing of principles and ordinances such as those found below. These simple steps necessary for redemption have been taught by prophets down through the ages. The most fundamental and redeeming principles are familiar to every Latter-day Saint: faith, repentance, baptism, and the gift of the Holy Ghost. These principles are taught throughout the scriptures. When these four are followed by priesthood ordination, the temple endowment, and temple sealing, one is prepared to endure in obedience while practicing and perfecting the virtues of love, service, humility, and so forth. The redeeming principles and ordinances as outlined have been taught since the time of Adam (see D&C 29:42) and are consistent across each dispensation of the gospel. (For the plan as taught by Enoch and Noah, see Moses 6 and 8.)

Steps Necessary for Redemption

- Faith in the Lord Jesus Christ
- Repentance
- Baptism
- The Gift of the Holy Ghost
- Ordination to the Melchizedek Priesthood
- Temple Endowment
- Temple Sealing
- Enduring in Obedience

It is interesting to note that the terms used to describe these principles have taken on different shades of meaning in their general usage in the Church. For example, a reference to the term "plan of salvation" in a Sunday School class would generally be followed by a discussion of where we come from, why we are here, and where we are going, accompanied by a blackboard illustration of circles representing the premortal existence, the mortal existence, and three degrees of glory. The fact that this is so is a testimony to the power of visual representation of a concept and the ability of such a representation to establish a definition in the minds of millions who have sat in Sunday School classes. In a similar vein, the term gospel is used primarily by Church members in the context of the New Testament teachings of the Savior during His mortal ministry and secondarily as a catchall term covering everything taught in the Church today.

Elder M. Russell Ballard has chosen to place emphasis on the term *plan of happiness*. This is a wonderful phrase for communicating to the world at large that a plan does exist whose purpose is to help us live useful, fulfilling, and happy lives.

Of course, the purpose of discussing the general usage of these terms is not to get bogged down in semantics but to develop a clear understanding of what it is that priesthood leaders should teach. The notion is straightforward. Priesthood leaders should teach fundamental principles and ordinances necessary for the salvation of members of the Church in this dispensation. When the plan of redemption is set in the context of this dispensation, we must add to the steps necessary for redemption at least the following: 1) the role of the Prophet Joseph Smith; 2) the Book of Mormon or a second witness of Christ; 3) the Apostasy and the Restoration; 4) continued revelation; 5) other Restoration scriptures—the Doctrine and Covenants and the Pearl of Great Price. Certainly the doctrine and principles outlined in Figure 2 are not meant to be exhaustive or all-inclusive. To arrive at a canonized list of "doctrines" or a descriptive term applied to the list that all must agree on is not the point. It is important to know that there is a "plan" and that the plan encompasses some simple principles and ordinances that are for the benefit of Heavenly Father's children.

I would like to pause here for a moment and encourage you in a particular direction. I believe this is such an important issue that if I were a bishop, stake president, quorum leader, or father, newly called (or otherwise), I would determine that those whom I led and loved would at some time in my ministry hear me speak and bear testimony about each principle listed in Figure 2. Wouldn't it be wonderful if for each principle you would keep either a written outline or a full text (this depends on one's style of speaking) in a three-ring binder as evidence to yourself that you had done your best to fulfill the scriptural mandate to be a teacher of the plan of redemption. These outlines or texts, well prepared, could be referred to over and over in the many different settings encountered by a priesthood leader in the course of a lifetime. They would be a wonderful heritage and written testimony to children and grandchildren. Most important, they would prepare the priesthood leader to teach eternal principles with power and effectiveness.

What Is to Be Accomplished by Teaching the Plan of Redemption

What is it as priesthood leaders we wish to accomplish by teaching the plan of redemption? An obvious response would be: We teach the plan in order that those who hear

Figure 2

The Plan of Redemption

In any dispensation:

- Faith in the Lord Jesus Christ, Godhead, Atonement, Resurrection

- Ordination to the Melchizedek Priesthood

- Endowment ordinance in the temple

- Repentance, godly sorrow for sin

- Sealing ordinance in the temple

- Baptism by immersion for the remission of sins

- Endurance to the end in obedience

- The Gift of the Holy Ghost

In this dispensation—additional principles:

- Role of the Prophet Joseph Smith

- The Book of Mormon as Another Witness of Jesus Christ

- The Apostasy and the Restoration

- Other Restoration Scriptures—The Doctrine and Covenants and the Pearl of Great Price

- Continued Revelation

and follow might be redeemed—might understand the principles and receive the redeeming ordinances that will allow them to return to the presence of our Heavenly Father. Alma the Younger in the 5th chapter of Alma said it beautifully and succinctly. "And behold, he [Alma Senior] preached the word unto your fathers, and a mighty change was also wrought in their hearts, and they humbled themselves and put their trust in the true and living God. And behold, they were faithful until the end; therefore they were saved."

It would be the hope of every priesthood leader that the teaching of redeeming principles would bring about a mighty change of heart in those who listened; a change of heart that would lead to repentance, that would lead to trust in the Lord and to faithful obedience to His commandments. Such a change of heart was clearly contemplated as the essence of a new covenant the Lord would make with His people. We read in Jeremiah:

> Behold, the days come, saith the Lord, that I will make a new covenant with the house of Israel, and with the house of Judah:
>
> Not according to the covenant that I made with their fathers in the day that I took them by the hand to bring them out of the land of Egypt; which my covenant they brake, although I was an husband unto them, saith the Lord:
>
> But this shall be the covenant that I will make with the house of Israel; after those days, saith the Lord, I will put my law in their inward parts, and write it in their hearts; and will be their God, and they shall be my people (Jeremiah 31:31–33).

The purpose of teaching the plan is to turn the hearts of listeners to Christ and to instill in them a desire to keep His commandments. Fundamentally, the doctrine is taught to achieve a change in behavior. Alma the Younger understood the concept well. At the beginning of the reign of the judges he had been appointed chief judge (an administrative as well as a judicial office) and also held the office of high priest over the Church. In year eight of the reign of the judges "the wickedness of the church was a great stumbling block to those who did not belong to the church; and thus the church began to fail in its progress." He was much troubled by what was happening among his people, but the scriptures report that despite his being very sorrowful, "the Spirit of the Lord did not fail him" (Alma 4:10, 15).

In other words, he did not get discouraged and quit but instead was inspired to make an interesting decision. In the beginning of the ninth year of the reign of the judges he gave up the judgment seat and had another man appointed in his stead. Alma 4 verse 19 explains why. "And this he did that he himself might go forth among his people, or among the people of Nephi, that he might preach the word of God unto them, to stir them up in remembrance of their duty."

Alma had worn two hats—one as an administrator whose time was spent in making and applying rules; the other as the presiding high priest. His inspired decision was not to spend more time trying to make and enforce more rules to correct the behavior of his people, but to speak to them of the word of God, to teach the doctrine and have their understanding of the plan of redemption lead them to change their behavior. Of course, the administrative side was not left undone, because another was appointed in his stead. But he chose to recognize his role as a priesthood leader and understood that his first responsibility was to teach faith and repentance to the people.

It's of some interest to note that fifty-three years later, in the sixty-second year of the reign of the judges, Nephi, who was Alma the Younger's great-grandson, did exactly the same thing. We are told "And it came to pass that

Nephi had become weary because of their iniquity; and he yielded up the judgment seat, and took it upon him to preach the word of God all the remainder of his days" (Helaman 5:4).

At work here is a very important pedagogical concept. It is that perhaps the most effective way to change behavior is to teach *doctrine,* from which emerge *principles* which, when understood, lead to *behavior.* It is important for leaders to remind themselves that it is difficult, if not futile, to force someone to do something. Agency is indeed part of the plan. The best approach is to teach the doctrine, enumerate the principles, and describe the desired behavior. Elder Boyd K. Packer has observed that "The study of the doctrines of the gospel will improve behavior quicker than a study of behavior will improve behavior" (*Ensign,* November 1986, p. 17). Figure 3 illustrates this concept.

Figure 3

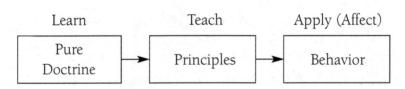

Learn	Teach	Apply (Affect)
Pure Doctrine	Principles	Behavior

Sometimes leaders wishing to achieve certain outcomes spend time and energy chiding, hectoring, and railing on the behavior of their people. This notion is certainly applicable to the parent-child relationship. Parents can spend their time nagging in the behavior box when more attention to principles and doctrine could yield better long-term results. A stellar example of this fundamental concept is found in the Church's welfare handbook, *Providing in the Lord's Own Way.* This is an exceptional document because it is principle based.

A "Strategic" Reason for Teaching
the Plan of Redemption

I have made the argument from the scriptures that the fundamental responsibility of priesthood leaders is to teach the plan of redemption. There is another reason, a "strategic" reason, why this notion is so important. Consider, if you will, the fundamental nature of the Church. At its foundation this is a *spiritual* work. It is true that the Church has evolved into a complex social organization that responds to a variety of needs. It is the nature of organized man to pursue shared goals and objectives. We are no different in the Church. We define ourselves in terms of sacrament meeting attendance, baptisms per missionary, number of Melchizedek Priesthood holders, ordinances, and so on, and that is appropriate. When it works at its best we see marvelous progress in the lives of organization members.

But the problem comes when the organization objectives overwhelm and take priority over the need to spiritually feed the individual members of the Church. Thus it is important that priesthood leaders accept that their number one priority, first and foremost in time, attention, and attitude, is to teach the plan of redemption. Organizational objectives are subordinate to the teaching of spiritual principles. This is a spiritual work. It is in the disseminating of spiritual truths that we have our greatest comparative advantage. President Ezra Taft Benson observed: "This latter-day work is spiritual. It takes spirituality to comprehend it, to love it, and to discern it." (*Come unto Christ* [Salt Lake City: Deseret Book, 1983], p. 23.) Other organizations can provide social, recreational, brotherhood, and sisterhood opportunities, and so on, at least as well as we. But we have the restored principles of spiritual salvation, taught by

authorized priesthood bearers under the direction of the
Holy Ghost. That is our comparative advantage over all
other organizations, religious or otherwise, and the teaching
of spiritual truths must be our explicit, reaffirmed, constant,
number-one priority.

Importance of Spiritual Conversion

Two very important considerations accompany the
strategic need to concentrate on the spiritual "comparative
advantage" aspect of this work. The first of these is a "big
picture" or "macro" reason. When the principles of the plan
are taught, whether in large groups or on a one-on-one
basis, a spiritual conversion needs to take place. While the
gospel is wonderfully logical, logic alone will not serve in
this case. Each individual being taught needs to be converted by the Spirit. One can understand the logic of a plan,
the need for authority, the principles of justice and mercy,
but still not be converted to them. How much more difficult
it would be, without a spiritual conversion, to embrace the
principles of the divine birth of Jesus Christ and His infinite
atonement. The teaching of the plan of redemption must be
done by the Spirit if conversion to macro principles is to be
accomplished.

Section 50 of the Doctrine and Covenants makes the
point quite clearly. In verse 13 we read, "Wherefore, I the
Lord ask you this question—unto what were ye ordained?"
In verse 14 we read the answer. "To preach my gospel by
the Spirit, even the Comforter which was sent forth to teach
the truth." So we teach by the Spirit in order for the plan,
the doctrine, the principles to be understood—in other
words, to get the big picture across.

The second reason for teaching by the Spirit is a "little
picture" or "micro" reason that embraces a concept whose

importance cannot be overstated. In fact, this concept is really at the heart of the challenge facing the Church today and should be understood by every priesthood holder. Let me explain the concept and then provide, in lieu of a story, a conceptual diagram and a reference to the Internal Revenue Service.

The gospel embraces millions of individuals who are each given agency to act independently in their own sphere. These individuals each have thousands of individual circumstances which must be accounted for. No set of written policy instructions can possibly embrace the myriad sets of circumstances that face each child of God who struggles to return home. How absolutely essential it is that macro *principles* be taught by the Spirit as *guidelines,* and micro *decisions* be made by the Spirit as practical *application.* Because of the complexity of life and the number of individuals involved nothing else will really work.

To amplify this notion, consider that it is easy to decry the deterioration in society that seems to be taking place at all levels. Because of the disintegration of the family, dishonesty, child and spouse abuse, crime, and so forth, much has been said about a need to return to fundamental values. No one should have to be convinced of the need for such a revisiting.

A parallel observation made with equal frequency has to do with the rapidity of change in our environment in general—change in technology, explosion in the amount of information available, re-engineering of the corporation, and so on. It is clear that all organizations struggle to keep up with rapid changes. It would be an enormous struggle for the Church if our response were to develop a new program for every new challenge faced by each constituent group in the Church. We cannot expect to be successful in that mode.

Figure 4 is a representation of the problem.

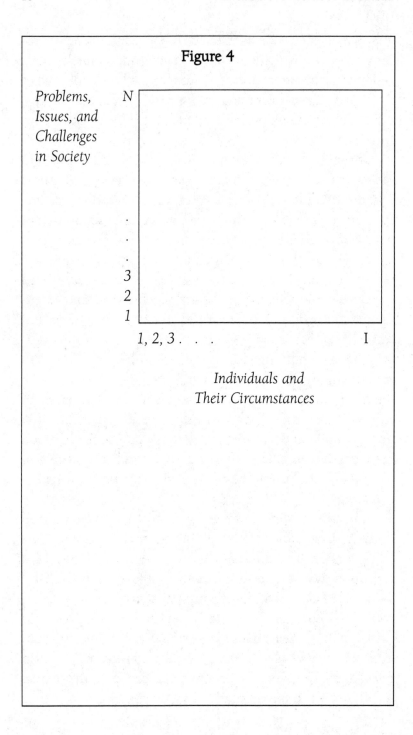

Figure 4 depicts a matrix in which the "X" axis represents the number of individuals (I) and their circumstances, and the "Y" axis represents the number of problems (N) that an individual could encounter.

The number of combinations of issues, problems, and challenges faced by individuals with particular circumstances is given by the number of boxes in the matrix. We know by experience and observation that I and N are both very large numbers. The total possible number of individuals and problems is given by multiplying I by N. So, for example, if there were only 1,000 people who had problems and just ten different kinds of problems, there would still be 10,000 variations of people and their problems [10 times 1,000=10,000]. Of course the numbers are more like billions of people and millions of problems!

Now, the challenge is straightforward. It is not possible or desirable to prepare a manual that spells out a specific answer for each of the I individuals who faces each of the N problems. In the Church, with millions of individuals and who knows how many different kinds of problems, it would require a manual of hundreds of millions of paragraphs to give specific counsel to each person and each problem.

Here's where the IRS manual provides such a convenient illustration of the problem and the difference in approaches. The IRS guidelines provide tens of thousands of paragraphs about how income and expense items ought to be determined for any conceivable situation. Schedule D alone could be responsible for severe cranial vapor lock. On the other hand, the Lord's law of finance—tithing—is defined as a simple principle: 10 percent of one's increase, and the details are left between the individual and the Lord.

The clever reader will say, "Wait, we'll simplify by grouping both individuals and problems." It is a good idea. Experience tells us that people are somewhat alike and problems can be generalized. We may aggregate or combine in either dimension by selecting like issues or like individuals and applying some prescription for improving their circumstances. So, for example, we could group all individuals who are not married into a group called "singles." We could identify the problem as "whether or not to marry," and the counsel would be: all single (non-married) individuals ought to face up squarely to the issue of marriage—and get married. The problem is obvious. We cannot be clever enough in aggregation in either dimension to spell out policies and programs to cover every contingency. Furthermore, we know it would be wrong even if it were possible, because it would abrogate the principle of moral agency.

To reiterate what was said several pages ago, no set of written policy instructions can possibly embrace the myriad sets of circumstances that face each child of God who struggles to return home. Therefore, it is inspired policy and correct organizational strategy as well as essential doctrine that the plan of redemption and its macro *principles* be taught by the Spirit as guidelines, and individual micro *decisions* be made by the Spirit for practical application.

Implications for Priesthood Leaders

There is an interesting implication for priesthood leaders in the notion that their number one responsibility is to teach the plan of redemption. It has to do with how they spend their individual and personal time. It is clearly related to the concept that the comparative advantage of the Church over other organizations is in its spiritual and doctrinal base. To maximize the spiritual and doctrinal advantage, it is necessary that priesthood leaders allocate a portion of their time to studying the doctrine and seeking the Spirit. This seems such an obvious principle, but it is more honored in the breach than in the observance. The difficulty is both practical and conceptual. The practical problem is that there are always other tasks that appear to have more immediacy. Delegation, follow-up, reorganizing, calling, counseling, and problem solving are necessary and useful tasks. They generally are given priority over our own in-depth study of spiritual topics. We cannot be faulted for seeking to serve others and performing tasks that accomplish that purpose. It is important, however, to find a balance between giving someone a fish and teaching someone to fish. That is the conceptual issue. Not only must the priesthood leader have knowledge of the doctrine and principles that must be taught, but he must teach them by the Spirit. Teaching by the Spirit requires being "in tune" with the Holy Ghost. This is a critically important notion and much has been written and said about it.

I would add this idea. I believe that one way to be in tune with the Spirit is to honor, revere, and hold in awe our Savior, Jesus Christ. When we feel this way we become "in tune" with the Holy Ghost because He knows, understands, sees, and *feels* that better and more profoundly than anyone else. Sometimes when we meet someone we speak of him or her as a "kindred spirit." Generally it is because our ideas, our aims, our interests, our loves and passions are the same. So it is with "the Spirit," whose purpose and interest is to testify of Christ. We can be "in tune" with the Holy Ghost when we share similar feelings about the Savior, when we have reverence for life and the Creation, and when it is our aim to testify of these things.

As suggested in the previous section, we live in an extraordinary, complex environment with all the complicated personal challenges that accompany that environment. Priesthood leaders must recognize that teaching doctrine and skills related to spiritual insight may have more long-run benefits than benefits received from the immediate problem solved. But effective teaching requires that the priesthood leader himself has invested time in studying, pondering, and praying.

To achieve the correct balance requires periodic assessment of personal time spent as well as time spent in meetings the leader is responsible for.

Where to Begin Teaching the Plan of Redemption

If the number one priority and responsibility of every priesthood leader is to teach the plan of redemption, is there a logical place to begin? There certainly is, and it is obvious as well as logical—we begin at home. Where do we begin in fulfilling the mandate of God that Melchizedek Priesthood leaders be teachers of the plan of redemption? We begin with ourselves and our families. So how do we teach the plan? We can read together from the scriptures, pray together, attend our Church meetings, hold family home evening gospel discussions. But wait a minute! This is all sounding very familiar. This sounds like counsel we have received continuously for decades. It is indeed, and the veracity of the counsel hasn't changed and won't change.

On occasion someone will approach me and observe that their family are holding family prayer, scripture study, home evening, and so forth, but that it doesn't seem to be doing any good. The older children are rebellious and there's more often a bad feeling than a good feeling. What follows is usually a visit about the relative merits of agency, the value of patience, and how to maintain a sense of humor—the principles our children excel in teaching us. But sometimes I will ask the question, "Why do you hold these activities?" The answer invariably is, "Because we've been told to by the Brethren." So I ask, "Why have the Brethren told you to?" The answer is, "Well, can I get back to you on that?"

But there is a serious point to be made here. It's easy to focus on activity or its mechanics and lose sight of the purpose. The suggestion is that the number one responsibility of every priesthood leader is to *teach* the plan of redemption. The number one priority for that teaching is to teach the family. So what are the best vehicles to teach the plan to the family? Certainly scripture reading, family prayer, Church meeting attendance, and so forth would be on the list.

Unfortunately, the model we have is the father administrator who convenes the meeting and "administers" by calling on the mother to do something. The model suggested by the scriptures is the father loving-teacher model; the father who understands faith and wants to teach it as one of the principles of the plan of redemption so that the children can be redeemed. This is the father who *teaches* every principle in the plan of redemption because that is his number one responsibility as a Melchizedek Priesthood holder, a priesthood holder who was known to his Heavenly Father and ordained to that purpose—to teach the plan of redemption! Of course the father-teacher model is that model used by our Heavenly Father. The plan that would keep track of everybody and guarantee their return was rejected. The plan of teaching principles and exercising moral agency was accepted. The challenge for parents is to put as much time and energy into inspired teaching of eternal principles as we put into administering our human wisdom and parental will.

After teaching the plan to our family members, what is the next priority? The initial response is almost always to say "to our friends and neighbors." There's no question that teaching the plan of redemption to friends and neighbors is important, but there is another category to whom our attention must be turned first. In section 88 of the Doctrine and Covenants we read (verse 77), "And I give unto you a commandment that you shall teach one another the doctrine of

Figure 5

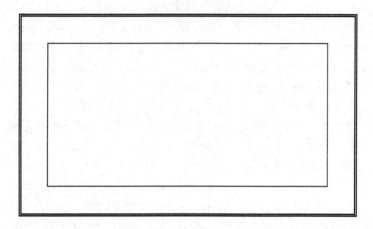

Figure 6

the kingdom." In our modern setting we are "aggregated" to one another in quorums, wards, and stakes. Each of these aggregations has a "priesthood leader." What is the number one *leadership* responsibility of each priesthood leader? To teach the plan of redemption. What is the number one *leadership* responsibility of the stake president? To be the stake's best teacher of the plan of redemption. The bishop? To teach the plan of redemption to his quorum members and ward members. The quorum president? To teach the plan of redemption to his quorum members. The emphasis here is obvious. The priesthood leader is defined first and foremost as a *teacher* of the plan. The challenge for quorum, ward, and stake leaders is similar to that of parents. It is to put as much effort into inspired teaching of the plan as is put into administering programs.

I can't resist the urge to insert here another conceptual diagram. It has to do with why we are to teach doctrine in the home and then teach it again "to one another" at church. The straightforward answer is of course "complete coverage." To illustrate, consider a lawn. Suppose it has a rectangular shape and the objective is to fertilize it with a drop spreader. The instructions on the package suggest that one begin by running the spreader all around the exterior of the rectangle to form a "header strip." (See Figure 5.)

Next the instructions suggest that the user run the spreader back and forth in parallel strips, being careful to overlap the wheels on each succeeding pass. (See Figure 6.)

Now the lawn is completely fertilized, and within a few days it will be uniformly green and beautiful, right? Wrong! Experience instructs that no matter how carefully the spreader is managed, following the above procedure will produce a lawn with stripes where the overlap was not quite right or the spreader didn't function efficiently. A further review of the instructions suggests that the "stripes" problem may be eliminated by running the spreader in a second pass perpendicular to the first. The result is a checkerboard pattern shown in Figure 7.

Figure 7

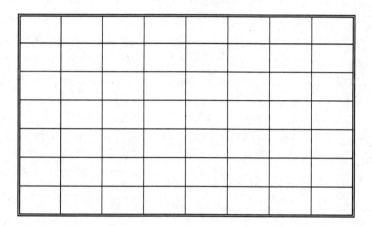

What does this have to do with teaching the plan of redemption? If every family in the Church were headed by a Melchizedek Priesthood leader and a companion who together taught vigorously and efficiently in the home, there would conceptually be "complete coverage." In such a setting every member of the Church would be taught correct principles. In fact, the conditions for complete coverage on one pass do not exist. There are many families with ineffective or non-existent Melchizedek Priesthood leaders. Thus the injunction that we teach one another in quorums is equivalent to running the spreader in a second pass perpendicular to the first pass in order that everyone, regardless of family structure, be taught correct principles. (See Figure 8.)

Figure 8

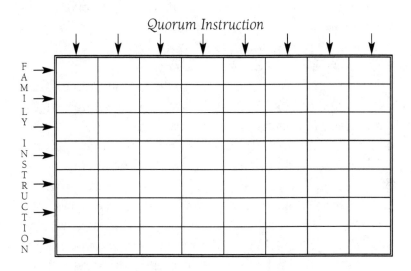

The benefit of this arrangement is that gospel principles are taught in such a way that hopefully no one falls through the cracks. This example makes explicit our understanding that priesthood leaders wear two hats—teacher of the plan of redemption in the home and teacher of the plan of redemption in the quorum. It also makes clear one of the Church's most serious challenges. It is to make explicit to every parent that the existence of a "second coverage" safety net should in *no way* be construed as a reason to abdicate the responsibility to teach correct principles in the home.

The third priority is in fact to teach the plan to friends and neighbors. Throughout history, those who have been recognized as leaders in the Church have been deeply involved in missionary work. The early Apostles, all of the Book of Mormon prophets, the early leaders of the Church in this dispensation—all have recognized the relationship between holding the Melchizedek Priesthood and teaching the plan of redemption to those who are not members of the Church. The modern injunction that every member is a missionary and that every young man should serve a full-time mission is the practical extension of the principle that teaching the plan of redemption is the foremost responsibility of every Melchizedek Priesthood holder.

In summary, leaders are those who epitomize the values of the group. The thing that is of greatest value in the Church is the doctrine and spiritual conversion to its principles. To be a "priesthood leader" is to teach and emulate the doctrines and principles that are the fundamental values of the group. A priesthood holder can manage programs and budgets, hold meetings and schedule interviews, preside and conduct, but he will not be perceived as a leader unless he teaches and lives the fundamental doctrine of the Church. Thus the first principle of priesthood leadership and first responsibility of every priesthood leader is to teach the plan of redemption.

May I invite you to do two things as you conclude reading this chapter. First, consider the Priesthood Leader Checklist that follows this paragraph. Ponder on each of the questions and consider the implications for your leadership style or practices. Second, take a moment and begin filling in the outline that was proposed in the introduction to the book. The first part of that outline is reproduced following the Priesthood Leader Checklist.

Priesthood Leader Checklist

1.____ Have I set aside time to study and understand the principles of the plan of redemption so I can teach them clearly?

2.____ Do I understand how to teach by the Spirit?

3.____ Have I taught the simple steps of redemption to my family members?

4.____ Is my model that of loving father, teacher, or that of dictator, enforcer, autocrat?

5.____ Do I teach the plan in sacrament meeting, leadership meetings, quorum meetings, ward and stake conferences, and interviews?

6.____ Do I live what I teach?

7.____ What else could I do to be a better leader/teacher of the plan of redemption?

Figure 1 (continued)

What Can I Do to Become a More Effective Priesthood Leader?

I.

    A.

    B.

    C.

CHAPTER TWO

MINISTERING

Bishop Grant Gunnell stands out in my mind as an extraordinarily effective priesthood leader. Every Church member should have a bishop like him.

We were a young family with two small children and had moved to California to continue our education at the University of California-Berkeley. We had moved into a small house in Pleasant Hill and were looking forward to getting acquainted in our new ward.

We had been in the Church building for only a few minutes when we looked at each other and said, "What is going on here?" We didn't realize it then, but we were about to learn the meaning of *hyperactive*. People were very friendly, everyone had a job and did that job. Sacrament meeting attendance, temple attendance, home teaching, and all other activity measures were higher than we'd ever seen them.

At the center of his hyperactive ward was Bishop Grant Gunnell. Why was it happening?

A few months later as a result of a small, almost insignificant incident, we began to understand why. It was Christmastime, and we stuffed our little family and all the presents into the Volkswagen and headed back to Utah for the holidays. We struggled over Donner Pass in a snowstorm and slipped and slid through Nevada. It was a typical winter trip and we didn't think much of it. We arrived in Manti late at night to the hugs and kisses of wonderful parents. We hadn't been there ten minutes when the telephone rang. It was Bishop Gunnell calling to see if we had made it home safely. We wondered: "Does the bishop call and check on everyone in the ward like this? How does he even know who our parents are or where they live? How did he get the phone number?"

Over time, we found that nearly every family in the ward could tell a similar story of the personal concern exhibited by this extraordinary priesthood leader who was *ministering* to the people.

Much has been said of late in the Church about ministering versus *administering*. As the Church grows in size and complexity there is a natural tendency for its leaders to think of themselves as administrators or managers. This self-perception is heightened by the number of programs in place that must be staffed, calendared, budgeted, monitored, and made to succeed. The list is very long: Primary, Relief Society, Young Men, Young Women, Boy Scouts, Elders quorum, High Priests quorum, Sunday School, Welfare, Family History, to name a few. Indeed it is quite remarkable that, given all that is to be administered, much of ministering still takes place in the Church.

Of course, it is true that well-run programs bless the lives of individual members of the Church. The purpose of every program in the Church is to help individual Church members in some aspect of their gospel living. Primary is organized to teach gospel principles to our precious children; the Aaronic Priesthood program is organized to help each young man learn his responsibility as a priesthood holder and to prepare to receive the Melchizedek

Priesthood; and so forth. There is not a program in the Church that is not designed to bless the individual lives of those to whom the program is directed. Slipshod or sloppy administering of any program will leave some one of us poorer for it.

But does administration constitute leadership? Is it in administering that priesthood leaders gain the power to move the people?

A very interesting insight into this question is provided by leadership studies involving a broad cross section of secular leaders. In such studies it is possible to use an analytical technique called multivariate analysis to determine empirically which are the most important factors of leadership. In such studies a wide variety of groups is examined. The purpose is to determine if there are factors that leaders of thieves, soldiers, athletes, plumbers, politicians, and so forth, have in common. The studies have demonstrated that leaders of all kinds share two important traits. First, leaders epitomize the values of the group, and second, they demonstrate concern for the welfare of group members. In other words, who do the thieves choose as their leader? First they identify the best thieves, then they choose from among them the one that demonstrates some concern for group members. Similarly the captain of the football team is usually an outstanding athlete who "cares" about the other players.

Isn't that interesting? Thieves, actors, accountants, football players, lawyers, businessmen characterize leaders not by their *administering* skills but by their *ministering* skills.

The results from such secular studies are helpful, but only because they corroborate the principles a priesthood leader observes in the peerless example of priesthood leadership offered by the Savior. For example, if the question were asked, What is the most salient or characteristic feature of the Savior's ministry, what would be the overwhelming response? The Savior is characterized, by those who adhere to His principles as well as those who don't, as first and foremost a great teacher. The New Testament account of Jesus' life among the Jews vividly portrays this aspect of His leadership. Indeed, Jesus is "the" great teacher in all of written history. As we know, He taught by both precept and example. The more believing people on the American continent found His teachings so powerful that in following them they experienced nearly two hundred years of peace and prosperity.

So the discussion in chapter one about the responsibility of priesthood leaders to teach the plan of redemption fits perfectly with the notion that leaders "epitomize the values of the group." In other words, in the Church of Jesus Christ "group," teaching the doctrine and living the doctrine is fundamental to leadership because the doctrine sets forth the values that the members of the Church espouse.

But in addition to leading by being a great teacher and follower of the doctrine, the Savior also demonstrated the second important leadership principle. It is that those who would lead in priesthood matters must also lead in ministering. This aspect of the Savior's mission—that He comforted, healed, and blessed them and took a very personal interest in the lives of those around Him—is a most compelling dimension of His life. In similar fashion, it should be a defining characteristic of each priesthood leader. There should be a willingness, even an eagerness, to use priesthood power to bless the personal lives of any with whom the priesthood leader comes in contact. In the terminology of the leadership studies, the leader is one who cares about the members of the group.

There are many tender and touching accounts of the Savior's love and His willingness to minister to the people. They are familiar to every student of the scriptures: the feeding of the five thousand, the healing of the blind and the lame, the comforting of the woman at the well, the raising of his friend Lazarus from the dead—these compassionate acts are remembered among countless others.

There is a particularly touching account in the Savior's
ministry that illustrates the importance He attaches to each
individual. In 3 Nephi we are told that "there were a great
multitude gathered together, of the people of Nephi, round
about the temple which was in the land Bountiful . . ." As
they were thus gathered the Savior appeared to them and
said: "Behold I am Jesus Christ, whom the prophets testified
shall come into the world. And behold, I am the light and
the life of the world; and I have drunk out of that bitter cup
which the Father hath given me, and have glorified the Father in taking upon me the sins of the world, in the which I
have suffered the will of the Father in all things from the beginning." (3 Nephi 11:1, 10–11.)

From the teachings of their prophets and from His presence, the people understood the significance of the Savior's
words. As a demonstration of their awe, wonder, and reverence "the whole multitude fell to the earth . . . And it came
to pass the Lord spake unto them saying: Arise and come
forth unto me, that ye may thrust your hands into my side,
and also that ye may feel the prints of the nails in my hands
and in my feet." (3 Nephi 11:12–14.) At that point the Savior could have chosen to hold up His hands, to point to His
side and to His feet, and to have the people see from where
they were that what He said was true. But this He chose not
to do. Instead the scriptures tell us, "And it came to pass
that the multitude went forth, and thrust their hands into
his side, and did feel the prints of the nails in his hands and
in his feet; and this they did do, going forth *one by one* until
they had all gone forth, and did see with *their* eyes and did
feel with *their* hands and did know of a surety." (3 Nephi
11:15; emphasis added.)

A few hours later Jesus repeated this example of

individual ministry when he blessed the little children. "And when he had said these words, he wept, and the multitude bare record of it, and he took their little children, one by one, and blessed them and prayed unto the Father for them" (3 Nephi 17:21).

And so the Savior chose to minister "one by one" to each individual in a very personalized and powerful way. He chose to take the time, to disregard any personal discomfort, to set aside other concerns and to "minister" to the people. What an extraordinary lesson in priesthood leadership!

Here is the major point. One can set guidelines, do budgets and reports, and monitor results, in other words administer or manage the blessing of lives by organizing others. It is not possible, however, to be a really effective leader without being personally and directly involved in ministering. *It turns out that our perception of what makes a person a leader, i.e., someone we are willing to follow, is inextricably tied with our understanding of how much he cares about us personally.* That caring has to be demonstrated by the leader's personal involvement.

It can be seen that the kind of leadership the Savior authored is well described by the two-factor leadership model. A priesthood leader should be one who epitomizes the values of the priesthood group and cares about its members. In other words, the most effective priesthood leader will be one who teaches the principles of the gospel in precept and in practice and who ministers to group members.

For many priesthood leaders, the acts that constitute ministering do not come easily. It is not that acts of compassion, thoughtfulness, and kindness are unnatural to them or must be performed unwillingly; it is rather that for most individuals a graceful and spontaneous caring must be learned and practiced. There are some individuals of both genders for whom such behavior seems second nature.

These are they to whom we gravitate in times of difficulty because they have a special ability to empathize, under-stand, and express love and concern. To be that kind of per-son, to develop the compassion and charity epitomized by the Savior, should be the desire of every disciple of Christ. To be an effective priesthood leader requires learning and practicing the Christlike love that expresses itself in acts of selfless service and priesthood ministry.

It is very important for priesthood leaders to appreciate that this quality of leadership cannot be artificial or con-trived. In other words, a priesthood leader does not "lead out" by "manufacturing" charity and performing insincere acts for "show." Genuine compassion can be developed if there exists in the heart of the individual, 1) a desire to be helpful, and 2) a willingness to try.

Desiring to Be Helpful

The desire to be helpful should be part and parcel of membership in the Church. As Alma was baptizing at the waters of Mormon he said to them, ". . . now, as ye are de-sirous to come into the fold of God, and to be called his people, and are willing to bear one another's burdens, that they may be light; yea, and are willing to mourn with those that mourn; yea, and comfort those that stand in need of comfort. . . . Now I say unto you if this be the desire of your hearts what have you against being baptized in the name of the Lord" (Mosiah 18:8–10).

Alma pointed out to his people that the desire to bear one another's burdens, to mourn with, and to comfort, were natural feelings that are associated with baptism and membership in the Church. These heartfelt desires to lift and buoy and strengthen are prompted by the spirit of the gospel and should be familiar to all Latter-day Saints, regardless of age or gender. Priesthood leaders should cultivate these latent feelings until they are spontaneous and a natural reaction accompanying their callings.

President Benson observed: "Spirituality, being in tune with the Spirit of the Lord—is the greatest need of Latter-day Saints. We should strive for the constant companionship of the Holy Ghost all the days of our lives. When we have the Spirit we will love to serve, we will love the Lord, and we will love those whom we serve." (*Come unto Christ,* p. 22.) His comment reminds us that a desire and willingness to serve is a natural offshoot of increasing spirituality. As we become better acquainted with the Savior—His doctrines and principles, His atoning sacrifice—and thereby become more in tune with the Spirit, we are led by that Spirit to a desire to serve.

Unfortunately the desire to be helpful can sometimes be stifled before any meaningful action is taken. There are occasions when a priesthood leader finds himself wondering what can be done that would make a difference. The natural tendency, perhaps for men more than women, is to want to see ahead to some result of an action or intervention. The inability to quickly perceive a course of action that has a predictable result can be a deterrent to beginning any kind of involvement. With some reflection and experience, however, we learn that it need not be so. Indeed, for an effective priesthood leader it must not be so.

One of the special blessings that comes to priesthood leaders is the opportunity to learn that the Lord will work *through* us as much as by us.

Often, as a General Authority, I had the opportunity to go with a stake president on Saturday morning visits to members' homes in stakes where I was assigned as a conference visitor. I enjoyed the visits very much but was always concerned that I had an obligation to accomplish something. After a number of experiences with visits to sick, inactive, widowed, and discouraged members, I learned an important principle. I don't believe the Lord expects us to go to people having in our mind a course of action and predetermined outcome. I do believe he expects us to go! And if we will make the effort to go to the homes of those who we think may be in need, He will work through us to bless the lives of others. He will inspire the right outcome. Indeed, I believe if we visit with the notion that "I will do something and it will be recognized as a good thing," we will miss an opportunity to be taught by the Spirit and have the Lord's will be done.

I remember a particularly interesting visit one wintry Saturday morning. We drove down a rural lane and came to a modest but comfortable home and knocked on the door. The door was opened by a lovely sister in her sixties, and beside her in a wheelchair was her husband. He was a large man with very large hands—the kind that seem to wrap twice around yours when you shake hands.

In the middle of the front room was a beautiful quilt tied on a quilting frame. I asked about the quilt and learned that a daughter was being married in six weeks' time and the tradition had been that each child when married would receive a special wedding quilt lovingly sewed by their mother. I asked how the project was going and learned that because of her arthritis the mother was no longer able to do the fine stitching required, and the task was now being undertaken by the father from his wheelchair. Even allowing for all his love and willingness, I realized that those very large hands were not well suited for quilting. He acknowledged he was making slow progress but was determined to keep trying.

We had a pleasant visit and went on our way. I didn't think much more about the experience, but later that Saturday evening, as I spoke to stake members in the adult session of conference, I was prompted to reference that visit as an example of loving and devoted parents who, in spite of some challenges, were maintaining family traditions and blessing their children—and I mentioned the quilt. A week later I received the following letter:

> Dear Elder Nadauld:
> Thank you for your help. The quilt is finished. The phone calls started coming in Sunday afternoon, and Monday the ladies started showing up with their thimbles. They came in "gangs" of two's and three's and by Friday the quilting was finished. One sister took it home to bind it and brought it back all done on Monday. There were nine ladies from throughout the stake who came to help (two we didn't even know). Several others called wanting to help but the quilt was done. I didn't think I would ever feel comfortable trying to quilt with a bunch of women but I worked right along with them. It has been such a *fun* and rewarding experience. Maybe next winter I should put on another one.
>
> Sincerely,
>
> Brother W.

In this instance, which began with just a desire to visit, there were multiple results. Of course a quilt was completed and presented to the newlyweds, but others were blessed to freely give of service and many were blessed to have another example of love in a stake. The Lord took care of the outcomes.

For priesthood leaders who are willing to try their hand at ministering, I think the Lord has in mind another very important outcome. Effective leaders draw strength from the people they lead. If they will associate with them and minister to them, leaders will be touched by the nobility of those who face great challenges with courage. Leaders will be buoyed up by the faith and goodness of their people. They will be blessed with humility and gratitude for their own weaknesses and strengths. Such feelings of humility and tenderness and empathy will improve the leader's vision, give compassion to his pronouncements, and teach him to lead with kindness and mercy.

In this context I think often of an example of a little eight-year-old boy. I believe his story and his inspiration are best told in his own words as he spoke from his wheelchair near the pulpit in the Sunday session of the Rigby Idaho East Stake Conference:

> One time there was a posse that was going after a bank robber. After following his tracks for many miles, they finally came upon the bank robber's abandoned wheelchair. The sheriff turned to his deputy and said, "Don't worry, he won't get far on foot."
>
> I'm Josh Shumway. I am eight years old. When I was born, I had a hole in my back. Because of that, I am paralyzed. I have been asked to speak on "How I fought the fight," but I decided to change that to "How I am fighting the fight," because I'm not finished yet. So far, I have had almost twenty surgeries, and I have more coming up. I don't like having surgeries, but I'm getting used to it. Heavenly Father *always* helps me feel comforted about it.
>
> Mostly, I want to tell you a little bit about my everyday life: I like to play baseball. I know I can't run around the bases, but I can propel myself around them by using my arms. I can go pretty fast that way. Also I can hit the ball pretty far, and I can catch, too. My brothers and my dad taught me how to pitch. I've used my arms so much to walk with my crutches and to move my wheelchair, that they have become very strong, so I can pitch and throw the ball hard.
>
> When we lived in California, my mom signed me up

to play T-ball. I was assigned to a team, but the coach of that team called my mom and said I could not play because I would slow down the pace of the game. My family and I really thought I could do it no matter what the coach said. My mom talked to the president of the league and he also thought I should not be allowed to play. It was a big disappointment because I really wanted to play . . . *bad,* and I knew I could do it if someone would just give me a chance. My family and I didn't give up. We prayed about what to do. We called every league in town until we found one who said they would love to have me in their league. One coach asked for me to be on his team. I did quite well on the team. I was able to play third base and the pitcher quite well. I got put out on first base quite a few times because it took me a long time to get there. But I did get there, eventually.

I tried not to think about the things I could not do. I thought about the things I *could* do. There were always lots of friends and neighbors at my games to cheer for me. Also, my parents and family came and encouraged me. My coaches always told me that *I could do it* and to keep on going. If all those people wouldn't have been there, I wouldn't have done so well. I probably would have quit. We all need other people to help us. Another reason I was able to do it was because the Lord was there. Sometimes I felt embarrassed or tired and then the still, small voice would tell me not to give up.

I know Heavenly Father loves me because he always helps me when I need him. I am learning that I have to accept myself the way I am. I have to accept that there are some things I'll never be able to do no matter how hard I try (at least until Jesus comes).

W. C. Fields once said, "If at first, you don't succeed, try, try again. Then give up. There's no use being a darn fool about it." We should never give up on anything easily, but we need to be realistic.

Football is one of the things I'd like to be able to do, but I'd rather not get myself killed. Obviously, I'll never be a track star either. Sometimes I feel sad about not being able to walk and run and play some sports. Sometimes I feel sad about it for a long time. Then I have to remind myself of all the things I *can* do. I remind myself that lots of people love me and always help me. I feel the love of my Heavenly Father and remember He is always there to support me. But the thing that gives me the most happiness and hope is knowing that Jesus is my brother and Savior. And I know I'll be able to walk when He comes. In fact, after He comes, I'm not going to stop running for a thousand years! When I think about what Jesus has done for me and what He will do for me, I feel so good. I can't wait until He comes again.

I hope all of you, when you get discouraged, will remember to think about the things you can do and never give up. I hope you will remember that Jesus and Heavenly Father love you and will always help you.

Who could not be inspired by the story of a boy with such courage and spirit? Those who would lead must reach out, seek to minister, and have their own souls touched in the process.

Forms of Ministering

Ministering can take many forms. Of course the kind of help that is offered should be tailored to the need and in all cases be directed by the Spirit. Providing sensitive and caring help is a skill that can be learned and improved upon. For example, it is a natural response to feel awkward in knowing how to comfort those who mourn the loss of a loved one. But the feeling of awkwardness or helplessness should be set aside and replaced by some form of contact and expression of caring. Appropriate responses may include a short personal visit, a telephone call or a letter, attendance at the viewing and/or funeral, and frequent contact in the lonely days that follow. These standard responses are a beginning. With some experience, skilled and sensitive priesthood leaders will see and hear and feel and be prompted to respond to more specific and individualized needs that exist in each situation.

Similarly, there are appropriate initial responses in the case of sickness. Visits to the home and the hospital and priesthood blessings are a beginning, but often there are children to be cared for, meals to provide, and house cleaning and other chores that may be done. Once the involvement is begun, other ways to bless and comfort will become apparent.

Death and illness are but two of the many kinds of trials that may be experienced. Those we know and love may be involved in drugs, alcohol, gambling, child or spouse abuse, criminal activity, or worse. The mere accusation of improper conduct can be devastating and wreak havoc on innocent individuals and their family members. It is so important in these situations that priesthood leaders proceed with a measured evenhanded response. Those in difficult situations should not be shunned or ignored. There are physical, spiritual, emotional, and economic needs that are legitimate and must be met. These simple human needs can be met without judgment. Kindness, love, and support in times of trial of any kind have no implication other than that the provider is following the example of Christlike love and compassion that every priesthood leader should wish to emulate.

Institutional Ministering

An appreciation for the importance of ministering in the Church has led to the development of programs whose intent is to organize the resources of the Church for more systematic responses. The home teaching, visiting teaching, and welfare programs are examples of organizing for systematic response. No one should doubt the importance of caring for the poor and the needy. The scriptural injunctions make it clear that this is both an individual responsibility and an institutional responsibility. The Church's welfare program has been and will continue to be one of the best demonstrable fruits of the restored true Church. Similar praise can be given to the home and visiting teaching programs, as through them countless lives are blessed.

Because these programs are so integral to the Church and to the concept of Christian living, it is imperative that priesthood leaders make them work. The Church will be a "leading" institution insofar as it devotes institutional resources to the care of its members. Similarly, individual priesthood holders will be "leaders" insofar as they devote personal resources to caring for those around them.

A note of caution: There is a risk to the Church in having well-defined programs for ministering. The risk is that individual members will assume that the organized program response is always working and is all that is needed. Of course, neither assumption is warranted. Organized responses provide opportunities and teach approaches, but true discipleship, true leadership, is evidenced by the spontaneous and individualized ministering that flows from the pure love of Christ.

Fortunately, examples of genuine, non-programmed ministry abound in the Church. They exist in every geography and at every level of responsibility. One of my favorite involves a member of the Quorum of the Twelve. He is one much admired for his intellect, administrative skills, and testimony of the work. About fifteen years ago I learned that a boyhood friend from Idaho whom I had loved and enjoyed very much had contracted cancer. He and his wife and family sought appropriate medical attention, fasted, prayed, and eventually drove to Salt Lake City and received a blessing from a loving Apostle whom he had never met before that visit. Over the course of the next few months, his condition worsened and he died leaving a young widow with four children.

The story could have ended there, after kind counsel, a blessing, and an outpouring of love and concern associated with the funeral. But it didn't. Over the course of the many ensuing years, the young widow and her children have been invited repeatedly to the home of the Apostle and have been blessed by his tireless ministering. Who could doubt that Apostle's leadership? Who would be unwilling to follow him?

Personal ministering is an integral part of priesthood leadership. The willingness to follow the Savior's example and personally bless individual lives distinguishes a leader from a manager or administrator. If one has the desire to begin and approaches the task with humility and charity, the way to proceed will be shown. The outcome can be left in the hand of the Lord, for it is, after all, His work.

As you did at the end of chapter 1, take a moment and ponder on the Priesthood Leader Checklist. Add to the outline introduced as Figure 1.

Priesthood Leader Checklist

1.____ Is ministering something that I do naturally or do I struggle in its application?

2.____ Do I have a desire to be helpful to others?

3.____ Do I look for opportunities to "practice" better ministering or do I avoid them?

4.____ If I made a list of things of a ministering nature that could be done, what would be on that list?

5.____ Is my ministering only in the form of responding to institutional assignments?

6.____ If I find it hard to care genuinely about others, what could I do to change?

7.____ Am I interested in learning how to minister in order to have the "prestige" of being a leader, or do I just want to follow the example of the Savior?

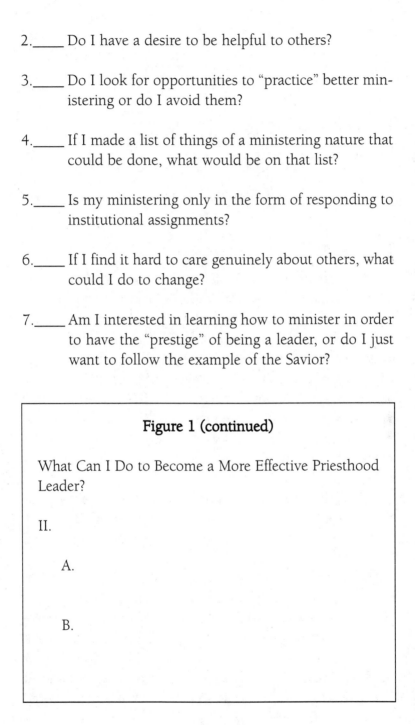

Figure 1 (continued)

What Can I Do to Become a More Effective Priesthood Leader?

II.

    A.

    B.

CHAPTER THREE

VISION AND FOCUS

Chapters 1 and 2 have focused on the priesthood holder as leader/teacher and leader/minister. When a priesthood holder is able to teach and live the plan of redemption and minister with love, he will be thought of as an effective leader in the Church. Indeed one cannot really be a leader without doing these two things well, regardless of what else one does. These two behaviors so define leadership that they may be thought of as fundamental and irreducible concepts for priesthood leaders at every level. These prin-ciples succeed at the quorum, ward, stake, or General Authority level.

Good Church leaders understand and practice the prin-ciples of teaching the doctrine and ministering. But really effective leaders go one step farther. It is that next step that is the topic of this chapter.

Let me share a very simple illustration. Some years ago my older boys and I had decided to climb to the top of Mount Timpanogos, which lies north of the city of Provo, Utah. We climbed to the small glacier-fed lake on the back side of the mountain, ate our lunch, and then began our climb to the top, where we could enjoy the magnificent view. We wrote our names in the log book and then headed north along the ridge. We worked our way to the top of the glacier that extended from the brow of the ridge all the way back down to the lake where we had earlier eaten our lunch. Here we found ourselves among a group of about thirty people who were milling around, looking over the edge of the glacier, and discussing the situation back and forth with one another.

As we got closer we could see the dilemma. The glacier fell away so steeply that it looked completely vertical from our vantage point on the top. There were no visible trails and none of us could see how we were going to make it off the ridge and down the glacier. We milled and discussed and considered for quite a while without making any progress.

Suddenly, out from the back of the group came a man in Levis, wearing cowboy boots and sporting a big Stetson hat. Without hesitation he walked up to the edge, held his hat over his head in his right hand, let out a big yahoo, and jumped straight out and over the edge. He landed on the seat of his pants, and as he slid down the glacier he made imaginary spurring motions with his cowboy boots. We were all completely captivated by this stranger who had suddenly become the leader. He had envisioned how to make it down the glacier. With his help we ceased our milling about, caught the vision, and followed him. We saw how it could be done and had a great time doing it.

In this chapter we will deal with a third principle that defines leadership. That principle concerns a trait that differentiates leaders from managers or any others in an organization. It is that leaders develop the ability to formulate or "catch" a vision of where the organization ought to go and what it ought to be doing. They can share the vision with others in the organization and then focus on the tasks necessary to accomplish the vision. This principle can also be stated as "Do the right things." In other words, *managers do things right, but leaders do the right things.* A leader can evaluate what is happening in the organization and realizes that there are generally a select few "right" things that if focused on by everyone will move the organization dramatically forward.

It is easy to illustrate this principle. When you are in a group of Church leaders, the question can be asked, "What did President Benson stand for, or what was the hallmark of his administration?" Before you can snap your fingers, the answer comes back almost in unison—read the Book of Mormon! President Benson understood that he could best "lead" by getting the whole Church to focus on one collective vision or idea. That vision was to read and follow the teachings in the Book of Mormon.

In a similar fashion, in less than a year, President Hunter led the Church to focus on two ideas, the temple and Christlike behavior.

This principle is important to the Church because it is an organization that wishes to accomplish something—to move a certain work forward. The Bible reminds us that "Where there is no vision, the people perish" (Proverbs 29:18). Much of an effective leader's time is spent in focusing the organization on accomplishing a few *right* things that get the organization where it is going.

The Church As an Organization

Certainly the organizational characteristics of the Church provide an interesting leadership challenge. All organizational members are volunteers—no one is paid for his efforts, so the traditional secular motivation of monetary reward does not come into play. A wide range of ability and commitment is displayed in any group of members. In addition, we really do believe in agency and we speak much of magnifying one's calling. For various reasons there is considerable turnover in the staffing of positions, which has significant training and leadership implications. We believe that everyone has the right and the responsibility to seek inspiration for his own calling, but we also believe that we should defer to the inspiration of someone in a higher calling. Thus a bishop is encouraged to seek inspiration to lead and guide the ward, but also to do as he is directed by the stake president. These interesting characteristics contribute to a wide range of leadership and management styles and responses. The continuum ranges from laissez-faire on the one end to a complete set of detailed instructions on the other.

Figure 9
Church Membership 1945–1995
(In Millions)

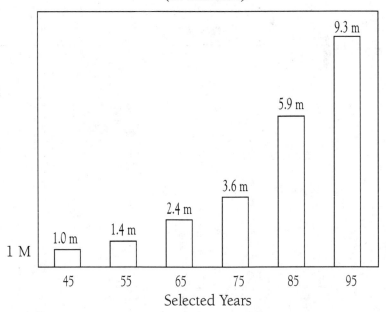

Source: *Deseret News,* Church Almanac 1997–98, p. 531.

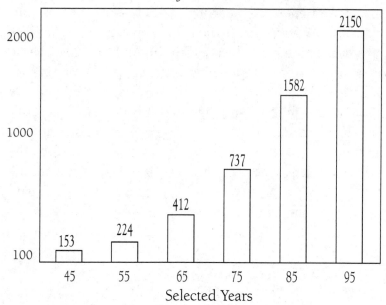

Figure 10
Number of Stakes 1945–1995

Source: *Deseret News,* Church Almanac 1997–98, p. 531.

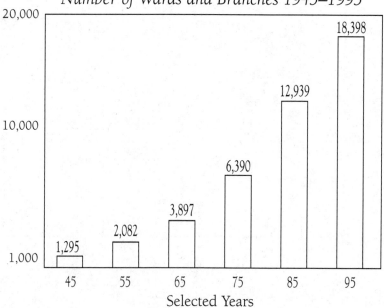

Figure 11
Number of Wards and Branches 1945–1995

Source: *Deseret News,* Church Almanac 1997–98, p. 531.

To add to the challenge is the issue of growth. The Church continues to grow dramatically in number of members, number of stakes, and number of units. Figure 9 shows the growth in number of Church members by decade since 1945. Similar data are shown for the growth in the number of stakes in Figure 10 and the number of wards and branches in Figure 11. In just the twenty years from 1975 to 1995, the number of wards and branches in the Church nearly tripled in number from 6,390 to 18,398. Of course, three times as many units require three times as many effective functioning leaders.

The growth of the Church by itself would necessitate an adjustment in management style. As organizations grow, there must be the inevitable shift from a largely centralized to a more decentralized approach. This would still be true if the organization were growing in a static environment. But that is clearly not the case. Not only is the Church experiencing rapid growth, but the environment in which it operates is becoming dramatically more complex. We have already addressed the doctrinal and teaching implications of that growth in chapter 1.

Finally, because the Church is an organization, we often and appropriately address ourselves to achieving measurable organizational objectives. One to which every priesthood leader can relate is the home teaching percentage. We keep track of sacrament meeting attendance along with activity measures for all the auxiliaries, and so on. Measuring our progress is a reasonable thing to do and is not incompatible with the mandate to teach the plan of redemption and minister to the needs of our brothers and sisters. Of course, it can be taken to extremes. Individual leaders can become overzealous and place tremendous pressure on everyone to improve the numbers, beat last period's performance, or achieve some numerical target. Unreasonable pressure from leaders can lead to all sorts of undesirable behavior that can compromise the integrity that needs to exist. The opposite end of the spectrum—where nothing is measured and leaders rely on good feelings and anecdotal accounts—results in an organization that is limp and under-achieving. Clearly this is an area, like every other, where balance must be sought.

So the leadership challenge is to take an organization that is religious, not secular, has volunteers, turnover, inspiration, diverse management styles, and enormous growth, and move that organization forward to accomplish something. The task would be impossible without a well-defined mission statement.

The Mission of the Church

Responding to the growth in size and complexity requires organizational leadership responses that provide clear signals to the organization in the same way that doctrine guides individual behavior. One such response that is extremely beneficial has occurred in recent years. It is the articulation of a clear statement of the mission of the Church with its threefold areas of emphasis. Clearly the hope is that Church leaders all over the world will be able to communicate that mission to members and invite them to participate in achieving it. Leaders of the Church everywhere should be familiar with the organizational vision of the Church—be able to articulate and share the vision. That's the essence of leadership at every level.

I observed firsthand, a wonderful example of this notion during a trip to the country of Haiti. In January of 1992 there was sufficient political unrest in Haiti that it was deemed wise to remove the missionaries from the country and reassign them to teach Haitians in southern Florida until stability returned. The transfer of the mission president and all the missionaries occurred very suddenly. As a result a young, native Haitian named Fritzner Joseph, who served as the CES coordinator, was called as mission president. His responsibility was to provide leadership to the members and carry on a missionary effort using local young men and women as full-time missionaries. President Joseph presided over the five thousand members of the Church in Haiti under very difficult circumstances.

For nearly three and one-half years it was not possible for any Church officials to visit the country. It was often not even possible to initiate contact with President Joseph by telephone. However, every two or three months circumstances were such that he could call out and report on the condition of the Saints. At one point we learned that food was badly needed for Church members. We managed to buy rice, beans, and other commodities in the Dominican Republic and deliver them in small family-size boxes to President Joseph. He in turn was able to drive throughout the country and distribute the boxes to one family and one house at a time.

Finally we deemed that it would be possible to visit Haiti and hold a combined district conference for the two member districts, which included eighteen branches. Elder Rulon Craven and I first met with the district presidencies and then held a Saturday evening meeting with as many of the adult priesthood holders and sisters as were able to attend. It is that meeting that so stands out in my mind. We wanted to gauge the organizational level and the gospel understanding of Church members who had been without outside influence or assistance for so long. Using my very rusty French, I began to ask this group of two hundred Haitian Saints some questions.

Are you able to hold your Church meetings? Oh, yes, we hold all of the meetings in the block schedule. Do you have elders quorum and Relief Society presidencies and Sunday School and Primary teachers? "Mais certainment!"—

which means, "well of course, Elder Nadauld." Then came the really impressive part. I asked, "What is the mission of the Church?" Almost in unison came the reply, "To bring people to Christ by perfecting the Saints, proclaiming the gospel, and redeeming the dead." Interestingly enough at about that point an electric failure caused the lights to go out, but nobody minded. They were accustomed to carrying on, and so we did. We had a wonderful discussion of Church principles without light to our eyes, but certainly with the light of the gospel filling our hearts and minds.

We were amazed. Without outside help or encouragement, and in very difficult conditions, President Joseph had managed to lead his people by communicating the mission of the Church in such a way that every member could articulate it and share in the vision it held forth. What a wonderful demonstration of leadership! President Joseph realized that he could accomplish something by having everyone share in the vision and mission of the Church.

But there is a practical problem facing leaders at the stake and ward level. The mission of the Church is broadly stated, and the structure of the Church includes a large number of organizations and programs. Figure 12 illustrates this notion. The upper part of the illustration shows the mission statement: "Come unto Christ" with the threefold emphases as *proclaim* the gospel, *perfect* the Saints, and *redeem* the dead. The lower part of the diagram attempts to capture the concept that there is a very large number of organizations and programs that stake and ward/branch leaders have to deal with. The question becomes—How can everything be improved and moved forward at the same time? In other words, how does a leader handle such a broad and aggressive agenda? It's a tough problem that leads to a significant amount of frustration among leaders. When this situation is presented to a group of priesthood leaders

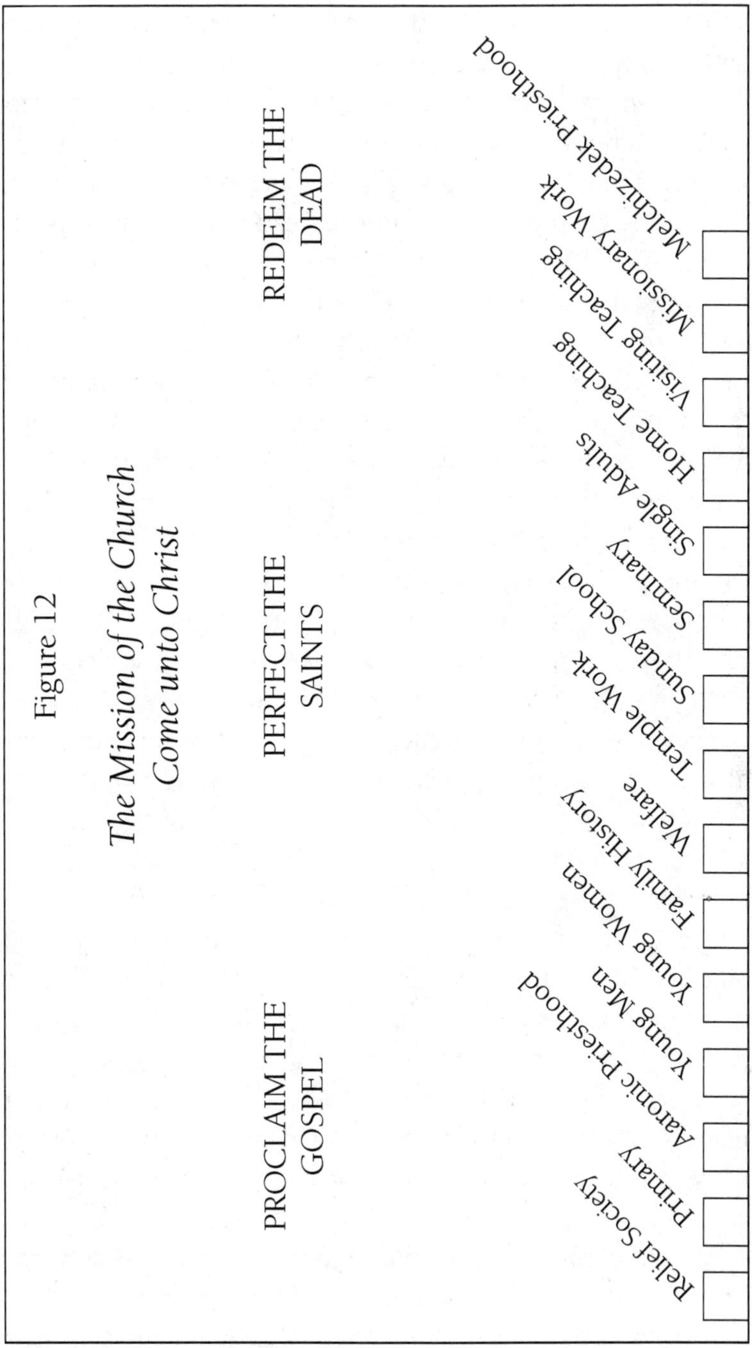

Figure 12

The Mission of the Church
Come unto Christ

PROCLAIM THE
GOSPEL

PERFECT THE
SAINTS

REDEEM THE
DEAD

Relief Society
Primary
Aaronic Priesthood
Young Men
Young Women
Family History
Welfare
Temple Work
Sunday School
Seminary
Single Adults
Home Teaching
Visiting Teaching
Missionary Work
Melchizedek Priesthood

and they are characterized as being spread "an inch deep and a mile wide," all the heads nod in agreement.

The "inch deep and a mile wide" problem is exacerbated by another interesting phenomenon. The wide variety of programs and organizations gives leaders at every level, from General Authority to quorum leader, a generous menu of things to "talk about" or train on. Thus at any leadership meeting a large number of different topics could be treated. We've all had the experience of going to a leadership meeting and coming away inspired and eager but with a list of ten things we need to do. The large number of possible topics and accompanying objectives leads naturally to a rapid bouncing over time from one objective to another. At each level of Church organization it's possible to have a "flavor of the month" approach to leadership. Programs and objectives can be introduced and then changed before meaningful progress can be made. To the number and frequency of changing objectives can be added the number and frequency of workers changing positions. The rapid turnover of individuals serving in callings coupled with a broad and ever-changing agenda makes a very challenging environment in which to operate.

Each of these factors affects an organization's ability to make meaningful progress. When there are many possible objectives to be pursued simultaneously, the typical result is that energies are so dissipated across the many objectives that progress is made on none of them. Most organizations (and people in them) have the ability to give attention to a relatively few objectives in any given time frame. When many are pursued all at the same time, nothing significant is accomplished in any one of them.

In the Church the result is shown when activity measures such as home teaching percentage, number of tithe payers, or sacrament meeting attendance are computed. For some units they consistently show no change over time. In other words, over a given period—say five years—there would be no sign of improvement in any of the measures that constitute a reading on the health or vitality of the quorum, ward, or stake.

Certainly in such a situation there would still be lives touched and individuals blessed by the efforts of leaders. In the absence of other data, it may well be the case that a ward or stake showing flat trend lines is doing well to "stay even." There may be factors that would produce significant declines if priesthood leaders were not exerting enormous effort to combat them. But generally the flat trend lines result from pursuing too many objectives at the same time or by constantly changing emphases. Large complex organizations are difficult to move. Starting, stopping, and changing directions cannot be achieved in a short time frame.

I have seen some remarkably able priesthood leaders tackle this problem. Let me give an example and then draw some principles from the illustration. Bishop Jones was a new bishop full of enthusiasm, but he had only lived in the ward a short time when called to his new position. He scheduled a ward council meeting and sent out notices in advance that for this meeting there would be only one agenda item, which he hoped the council members would consider and come prepared to discuss. The agenda item was, "What one thing could we do in this ward that would make the most difference to the most people in the ward."

The bishop and his counselors came to the meeting and, save for asking a few clarifying questions, spent the entire time listening to the discussion among members of the ward council. At the end of the meeting the council had generated a list of six things that they thought might be "most" important. The bishop instructed the council members to go home and do two things: first, after additional thought and prayer, narrow the list of six down to two and identify which of the two was really the more important;

second, give consideration to how the ward might measure its progress in either of the two areas and over what time period their progress should be measured. They were instructed that these two ideas would be the only agenda items considered in the next ward council meeting.

An interesting thing happened. When the ward council reconvened, the bishop found that after thinking and praying about their assignments the bishopric and three-fourths of the council members had the same item as number one on their list. The rest had that item as number two on the list. When the second council meeting had ended they had agreed on the one thing they were all going to work on, that they would work on it together for six months, and that they would measure their progress in a particular fashion that all agreed would be meaningful.

The bishop had met the organizational challenge facing most priesthood leaders. That challenge is to lead in the development of a shared vision of what the quorum, ward, or stake can achieve and to maintain the focus of the group on achieving the organizational goals that make up that vision. As that process unfolds, there are three constructs to keep in mind.

First, an effective leader has to be able to catch a vision of what the organization must do to be successful. In addition, that vision of what is to be accomplished must be shared by all involved. Second, because it is difficult for organizations to make progress on a large number of objectives simultaneously, the vision must be focused on a few well-defined and articulated objectives. Third, the vision of what is to be achieved must be measurable—not for anyone's aggrandizement, but for the purpose of providing meaningful interim feedback that can motivate everyone to keep working to bring the vision to pass. Each of these ideas deserves further development.

A Vision of the Work

"There is no more powerful engine driving an organization toward excellence and long-range success than an attractive, worthwhile, and achievable vision of the future, widely shared" (Burt Nanus, *Visionary Leadership*, [San Francisco: Jossey-Bass Inc., 1992], p. 3). Latter-day Saints as individuals share the belief that we can return to live with a loving Heavenly Father, and that view of the future is a significant motivation for personal progress. Enoch, as a great leader, had a vision of the future that inspired and lifted (literally) a whole city. A vision for an organization is a mental model of the future. It is a realistic, believable, and attractive view of what the organization may become and its people may achieve.

Having a vision of the work is necessary at every level of the organization. At each level there must be an understanding of the overall mission of the organization and a sense of the parameters and bounds within which that level of the organization can operate. Leaders conferring with each other and soliciting input from all others fashion a vision of the work that is consistent with the mission and the level at which they operate. Thus in the Church, the First Presidency and Quorum of the Twelve, sitting together in council and seeking inspiration, have defined and articulated the mission of the Church. Stake- and ward-level leaders counsel together, not to change or adjust the Church's mission but to envision together how that mission might be accomplished at the stake and ward level.

The leadership skill of being able to develop, shape, and articulate a shared vision of what can be achieved by those being led is the key factor in having the organization do the *right* things. To motivate excellence and progress, leaders must find the right vision from among the many possibilities that the organization may pursue. In the

Church the best forum for this is in the ward or stake council. The previously related example of Bishop Jones illustrates in simple terms how a ward or stake council can function as a vehicle for helping promote this leadership principle. A group of dedicated men and women who are led by an inspired bishop and who share a vision of the work can be so extraordinarily effective. Elder M. Russell Ballard's book *Counseling With Our Councils: Learning to Minister Together in the Church and in the Family* is an excellent resource designed to help leaders learn how to use councils.

There is great wisdom in the use of councils in Church leadership. Occasionally in organizations an individual emerges with such charisma, intellect, and force of personality that people will "follow him or her anywhere." History provides many examples, both good and bad, of charismatic leadership. In some cases the personality, willpower, and ability to articulate so captures people's imaginations that it overpowers the judgment and morality of otherwise good people. Leadership in the Church is not and should not become a personality cult. Obviously strong personalities put to good use are helpful. But it is very important that the vision of the work that emerges from Church leadership is one that focuses on building the kingdom of God on the earth, on supporting the already well-defined mission of the Church, and on giving the glory and honor to our Heavenly Father as His Son, Jesus, so often taught. (Jesus' intercessory prayer in John chapter 17 is a prime example.)

Sometimes leadership is assumed by someone who does not have a particularly forceful or even pleasing personality, but seems to gravitate to the role of leader because of technical expertise. A person who puts forth the effort to learn the rules, understands the complexities, and so on, is often in a position to assume leadership because it is easier for members of the group to "let George do it" than to learn the technicalities themselves. Leadership through a knowledge of rules, systems, and techniques is more management than leadership. The organization usually survives but may not thrive. It is stagnant, not vibrant, fails to inspire, and struggles to achieve. It has activity but no progress. It has management but not leadership. It lacks *vision*.

Conversely the right vision has the power to inspire and energize, to attract commitment, and to set new standards and lead the organization into the future. Really effective leaders sometimes intuitively, but most often through effort and inspiration, capture, share, and articulate a vision of the work that motivates and inspires. The process of forming and shaping the mental model of the future state of the organization usually begins by asking the right questions.

For example, leaders could start by asking questions such as: What are we doing well and what would we like to do better? These two questions and their answers address the strengths and weaknesses of the stake, ward, or quorum. Other questions might include: What are we being encouraged to do by our leaders? If we wanted to do just one thing but do it well, what would it be? What constraints (attitudes, resources, and so on) are keeping us from making measurable progress? The process of shaping a vision or model of a desired future illustrates a very important principle of priesthood leadership. The principle is that effort and inspiration go hand in hand. Most often inspiration comes after substantial effort.

Consider that members of a quorum, ward, or stake generally have a good idea about what is most needed to move the work forward in that particular unit. To get the benefit of that insight requires effort on the part of the priesthood leader. The process involves gathering members together, asking questions, and listening carefully. The listening step is especially important. It's important for two reasons. First, the purpose of the process is to learn how people feel, what they think is important to accomplish, and how they believe it can be done. Preconceived notions must be set aside and real listening practiced. Second, honest listening and understanding is the basis from which the leader obtains support for accomplishing tasks that ultimately must be assigned back to the members.

Here it is important to make a critical point. The process of soliciting input, of involving group members in understanding the needs of the organization and formulating a vision that can be acted upon, does not abrogate inspiration. On the contrary, it is by being involved in the process that a priesthood leader receives inspiration. Most of the sections of the Doctrine and Covenants came as response to pleas from the Prophet Joseph for help after he was deeply involved in the problem-solving process.

The experience of Nephi in the Book of Mormon is a classic example of getting involved in the process and then receiving inspiration. Nephi and his brothers had gone back to Jerusalem to obtain the brass plates. The first attempt was made by Laman, who approached Laban and made a straightforward request that they be given the plates. Laban called him a robber, threatened to kill him, and chased him away. In the second attempt, the brothers gathered up their gold, silver, and precious things and took them to Laban hoping to exchange their riches for the plates. When Laban saw their property, he simply took it from them and then sent his servants to slay them. With considerable effort and after timely intervention from an angel, Nephi was finally able to convince his brothers to try one more time to obtain the plates. And here's the key point. After two failed attempts and visitation from an angel, Nephi still did not know how he was going to accomplish the task. As he sneaked into the city to try for a third time, he says, "I, Nephi, crept into the city and went forth towards the house of Laban. And I was led by the Spirit, not knowing beforehand the things which I should do. Nevertheless, I went forth." (1 Nephi 4:5–7.)

It would certainly have been easier (not to mention less traumatic) if Nephi could have propped his feet up on the desk in his tent and had a course of action unfolded to him, but he had to be completely involved in the process. And then, during and through that involvement, the inspiration came. It is the same for priesthood leaders today. An elders quorum presidency, bishopric, or stake presidency that counsels together will do well. They will do best if they involve the ward or stake council and other members as appropriate in discussions as they seek information and insight. The whisperings of the Spirit generally come, as they did to Nephi, as the leader is fully involved in the process. From the process and from inspiration will evolve a shared vision that will provide direction, motivation, and commitment to move the work forward.

Focusing the Vision

Return to the example of Bishop Jones and note that in the process of counseling together, the ward council had generated a list of six things that they thought might be "most" important. With that thought in mind, consider again Figure 12 and the concept of focusing or "targeting" the vision. As Figure 12 depicts, the mission of the Church, to bring all unto Christ, is divided into three familiar parts: *proclaim* the gospel, *perfect* the saints, and *redeem* the dead.

These broad objectives must be kept in mind to ensure that our efforts do help achieve the mission of the Church. However, they are at too high a level of abstraction to provide measurable operational goals. As Bishop Brown intuitively understood, trying to move forward everything described on the bottom of Figure 12 and do it all at once puts the leader in the "inch deep and mile wide" difficulty referred to earlier.

What is needed is something in the middle, something aggregating but not too abstract. Consider Figure 13, which is a reproduction of Figure 12 but has the addition of several concentric circles and some lines with arrows. The concentric circles are meant to be thought of as bull's eyes, targets, or areas of focus. Note that the lines radiating out from the targets are labeled "collateral value." The purpose of the diagram is to illustrate a critical point in the leadership concept of do the *right* things. It is that leaders and members of a quorum, ward, or stake can choose one or two (at most, probably, three) areas of focus or targets that have the significant property of high "collateral value." Collateral in this context means supportive or corroborative. Thus choosing an area of focus with high collateral values means choosing to focus on something whose effect reaches out and supports other objectives.

The central notion is that a stake, ward, or quorum ought to concentrate or focus its efforts in several areas that have collateral value. In practice there are a limited number of areas that have significant collateral value. For example, one alternative may be to focus on the temple. Temple attendance requires that members be attending meetings, keeping basic commandments, paying tithing, etc., all of which have considerable impact on all organizations and programs of the Church. Other areas of focus with potential collateral value are outstanding youth programs, missionary work, Melchizedek Priesthood ordination, and home teaching. Obviously these areas of focus are all within the scope of the mission of the Church. While perhaps not necessary, the observation ought to be made that *any focus that does not directly support the mission of the Church is inappropriate.*

It would be nice if a leader could get organization

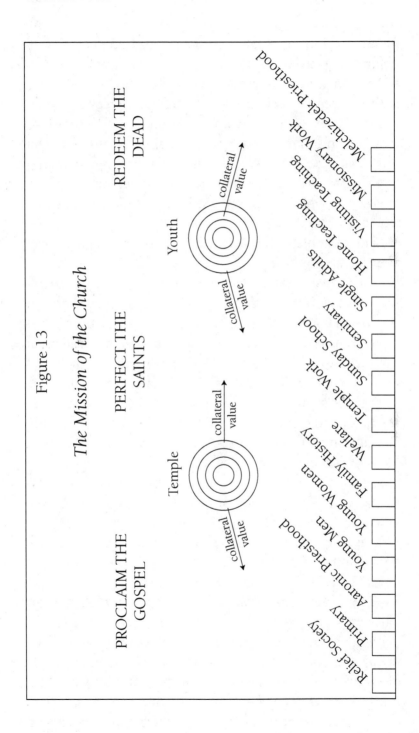

Figure 13

The Mission of the Church

PROCLAIM THE GOSPEL

PERFECT THE SAINTS

REDEEM THE DEAD

Temple

Youth

collateral value

collateral value

collateral value

collateral value

Relief Society
Primary
Aaronic Priesthood
Young Men
Young Women
Family History
Welfare
Temple Work
Sunday School
Seminary
Single Adults
Home Teaching
Visiting Teaching
Missionary Work
Melchizedek Priesthood

members to make progress across a broad number of well-defined objectives. In practice, a kind of "sensory overload" sets in when too many objectives are pushed. When faced with the complexity of modern living, which requires attention to career, children, community, professional, social activities, and so forth, and the myriad obligations that clutter one's calendar, the church is facing stiff competition for members' attention. It is much easier to get and keep that attention if there is a focus that is well articulated and maintained over time.

For example, stake president and stake members may, after the appropriate processing, decide that the vision they have for the stake is to be characterized as a "temple attending" stake with the "strongest youth program" in the area. If this vision and focus has been "bought into" by having had input from bishops, high council, and auxiliary leaders, it can serve as a powerful tool for capturing members' imagination, keeping their attention and motivating them to achieve the shared vision. The twin foci of temple and youth reach out and touch most aspects of member involvement.

Thus leaders help members to catch a vision and to focus on achieving objectives that have broad impact across the organization. These two leadership skills are critical to the success of any organization—the ability to gather the group together and help define and articulate a vision of what is to be accomplished, and the ability to focus everyone's efforts on a few carefully chosen objectives that will ensure the accomplishment of this vision.

The current organizational structure of the Church divides the world into geographical areas, each of which is supervised by an Area Presidency. Area Presidencies may be involved in the process of applying the leadership principle of vision and focus, and that involvement may vary from area to area. On one end of the spectrum, Area Presidencies may set forward a number of very precise and articulated objectives that they ask the stake presidents to accomplish. On the other end of the spectrum, they may invite stake presidents to counsel with their counselors, high council, stake council, and bishoprics and bring forward well-defined objectives that they wish to pursue. There is, of course, a middle ground.

At this writing, the Church is somewhat in that middle ground. In order to help stake and ward leaders focus on a few objectives with high collateral value, the Church introduced in 1995 the "Leadership Training Emphasis." The initial leadership training emphasis directed priesthood leaders to focus on 1) family spirituality, 2) temple attendance for adults, 3) missionary and temple preparation for youth, and 4) conversion, activation, and retention for all members. These four objectives are at a level of abstraction midway between the mission statement and the day-to-day programs and organization depicted in Figure 13. To communicate that these emphases would not change quickly, printed at the bottom of the training document is the statement, "This emphasis will continue until steady improvement is apparent."

Thus local leaders are encouraged to focus their efforts on seeing improvement in a few right things. Stake presidents and bishops are given the opportunity to gather together stake council and ward/branch council members and extend and expand that training emphasis (vision) into the operating fabric of the stake and ward/branches. The result of that effort should be an understanding of the value of pursuing the training emphasis and some well-defined (focused) objectives that can be measured.

Measuring the Vision

In order to be useful, the objectives that fall from a collective vision must be measurable. The notion of measuring to improve performance is pervasive, familiar, and widely experienced in secular endeavors. For the most part, measurement is embraced enthusiastically. This is especially true in athletic contests where keeping score is straightforward, often dramatic, and provides immediate feedback.

It is possible, however, to question the value of measuring in a religious context. Matters of the heart, the spirit, and the soul are difficult to quantify and appropriate objections can be raised when over-zealous application of measurement is made in these areas. That is why it is so important that leaders and members understand that the priesthood leader's first priority is to teach the plan of redemption and minister to members' needs. Needless resentment may result if the impression or reality is that the only concern is to quantify and press for measurement where intuition suggests otherwise. Our having said that, it remains the case that organizations and people in them are well-served by appropriate measurements. President Thomas S. Monson of the First Presidency has noted, "When performance is measured, performance improves, when performance is measured and reported, the rate of improvement accelerates" (Conference Report, October 1970, p. 4). It is well for priesthood leaders to keep track of sacrament meeting attendance, home teaching, and tithe paying among others. These and similar measures of the health and progress of a quorum, ward, or stake provide feedback to leaders and members that are important indicators of spiritual health. Without them it would be more difficult to know where to direct attention and effort.

They can be useful in another way. Organizations succeed by keeping members focused and continually motivated. The best use of data is in helping to maintain focus and in monitoring progress. The sharing of measured successes, even if only small ones, is the best way to keep the organization moving ahead to accomplish its goals.

There's no magic or an absolutely right way to measure progress in an organization. The principle is that the measured data ought to relate as closely as possible to the desired outcomes that have been envisioned by leaders. For large organizations it is difficult, confusing, and costly to continually make changes in the "accounting structure." As a result, the measurement process is not usually as precise as might be wished. Much time and effort can be wasted if each new leader develops his or her own system of measuring progress. Most often the needed data is already available in some form or can be made adequate with minimal changes and additions.

One might ask, What measures could be used to monitor the health and progress of a typical ward or branch unit in the Church? The straightforward notion is that certain activities could be measured at time zero and then again at time one (and subsequent periods) to see what changes may have occurred in the interim.

These changes can be measured in percentage terms or in simple additions to or subtractions from the beginning (bare) number. Percentage change is easy to compute and supplies familiar measures such as home teaching percentage or percentage of attendance at sacrament meeting. Sometimes the raw numbers are intuitive and more useful. Suppose a ward or branch of two hundred reports a 40 percent attendance at sacrament meeting. Leaders may talk of raising the attendance to 45 percent. However, it may be more meaningful to speak in terms of "wouldn't it be a blessing to have ten more people regularly attending sacrament meeting?" When stated this way there is more focus on individual people and less on a percentage number.

Here is a simple statement of the concept: If a stake president, bishop, or branch president were to look at the activity data for the Church unit he leads he would typically find three to five years of quarterly data on a dozen or so different measures. Review of that data that reveals no significant improvement in any important measure over time should give the leader reason to pause and take stock.

It has previously been observed that in such a case, classes have been taught, interviews held, principles enumerated, and lives touched. The issue here is that the organization has not been moved forward by a shared vision and a focus on a few objectives whose accomplishment would bless additional lives.

A vision and focused plan for the next time period might include first increasing the number (not percent) of temple recommend holders from X to X+30; second increasing the number of convert baptisms from Y to Y+10; third increasing the number of missionaries serving from the stake, ward, or branch from Z to Z+6.

Each of the proposed measures could be taken from existing membership data. In the example, each would relate to a specific leadership emphasis or focus: temple, measured by recommend holders; missionary, measured by convert baptisms; youth, measured by number of missionaries serving. Progress would be made by focusing on a few measurable objectives, maintaining the focus throughout a whole year or more and involving all appropriate leaders—stake council, ward council, quorum, auxiliary, and so on—in achieving the same shared vision. Interim reports could be passed along to help maintain the focus and generate enthusiasm that would come from the progress made.

For any Church unit real growth or improvement would be realized if at a specified future time there were more people attending sacrament meeting, more temple recommends held, more Melchizedek Priesthood advancements, more tithe payers, more convert baptisms, more families visited, and more missionaries serving. Of course, other measures could be employed and each may be useful to assess some aspect of the organizational health of a unit. Again, the principle is that the measurements should be kept simple and they should relate to the envisioned objectives.

Obviously the detail about how the stake presidency works with the high council, stake council, and bishops, and how the bishops work with quorums and auxiliary leaders, which meetings are held, what is said, and so forth, have not been discussed here. The principle is that effective leaders are those who can capture, formulate, or catch a vision of where the organization ought to go, share that vision in breadth and depth, and focus the organization on a few right things that can be accomplished and measured. The principle can be applied in many different ways, and results are best achieved when specific details are tailored to fit local circumstances and conditions.

In this chapter we have talked about a leadership principle I have called "Vision and Focus." It is really at the heart of effective leadership in any organization, including the Church. Teaching doctrine and the principles of the plan of redemption is a straightforward proposition. Ministering is a labor of love and service. But Church leaders also have the responsibility to move the work forward in measurable ways.

To do this requires at least three essential steps that we have discussed. Step one concerns a vision of the work. It is so important that leaders capture the energy and support of members by helping them "see" where the organization is going. This envisioning or mental modeling must take place at all levels. The overarching mission of the Church to bring souls unto Christ with its three-fold emphasis must be understood. But it is equally important that local leaders formulate a clear vision of what the quorum, ward, or stake can do in support of the leadership training emphasis. That vision needs to be developed and shared by local members and constitutes a clear picture of what collective energies can accomplish.

Step two involves the critical state of focusing the vision on a few specific, attainable aspects of the vision. Without focus the vision remains ethereal and the organization wanders through the inch-deep and mile-wide swamp that faces every complex organization. With focus the organization can see where to exert energy and will have a satisfying sense of accomplishment when the specific results are obtained.

Step three has to do with measurement. Measurement helps bring tone and tenor to the organization. It provides feedback for the necessary course corrections that are part of achieving any objective. It helps create enthusiasm as everyone observes the progress toward the envisioned end. It helps maintain organizational discipline and preserve focus.

Vision, focus, and measurement really work! In a nutshell the principle is that effective leaders are those who can capture, formulate, or catch a vision of where the organization ought to go, share that vision in breadth and depth, and focus the organization on a few right things that can be accomplished and measured. When dedicated Latter-day Saint leaders apply these principles to the work of the Lord, lives are blessed, the work goes forward, and enormous satisfaction is realized.

Priesthood Leader Checklist

1.____ Do I understand the mission of the Church?

2.____ Can I envision what I could do in my calling to advance the mission of the Church?

3.____ What group could help me capture a workable vision of what could be done?

4.____ How can I share that vision? In what settings? What language? Which examples would be useful?

5.____ What two or three specific things could be focused on?

6.____ Are the areas of focus defined as outcomes that can be measurable?

Figure 1 (continued)

What Can I Do to Become a More Effective Priesthood Leader?

III.

    A.

    B.

    C.

• CHAPTER FOUR •

AARONIC
PRIESTHOOD LEADERSHIP

I can still see it in my mind's eye. It was Sunday morning and there about twenty-five feet up in the top of the very large tree in our front yard was a big, strong, eighteen-year-old boy. He was wearing his Sunday clothes —white shirt, tie, nice pants. He was surrounded on nearby limbs by six or seven others in similar attire. Their most prominent features were the big grins they had on their faces.

I have no idea what our nonmember neighbors thought. I suppose it looked like a flock of very strange birds had swooped out of the sky and landed in our tree. They were having just as much fun taking the fifteen rolls of toilet paper out of the tree as they undoubtedly had putting it in the tree the Saturday night before.

This was not our first experience with that particular flock of priests. I had been the Young Men president and their quorum advisor for several years and had come to know them as an energetic (some would say wild), playful, and an altogether typical group of sixteen- to eighteen-year-old boys. Indeed, as I looked at the boy highest in the tree, I remembered a remark I had made to Margaret several years earlier—something about why didn't this boy's parents do a little better job with him? Of course, our own boys were then three and four years old, so we were in the best possible position to render an expert opinion on these matters. Now that Margaret and I have had seven teenage sons of our own, you can only imagine how many times I have eaten those words.

In 1997, nearly twenty-five years later, we saw that flock of priests again. One of them organized a reunion for us all. We met in Provo, at general conference time, at the home of one of the boy's parents. There was the former bishop and his wife, Margaret and I, and eighteen of the nicest Melchizedek Priesthood holders you have ever seen. They came from California, Oregon, Washington, Idaho, and Louisiana. They were Scoutmasters, bishops, and elders quorum presidents. They loved the gospel and they loved the Lord.

The boy highest in the tree? The ringleader? The one about whom I had said to Margaret: "I know he's a nice-looking boy, honey, but I think he's just a scatter-brained football player!" Yes, he was there. I knew he would be. Three years before, I had visited a stake conference in Louisiana with the assignment to reorganize the stake presidency. I had been told about a wonderful young counselor in the stake presidency who would have made a great stake president had he not just moved. He had been a professor at the university, had a national reputation in his field, and had been recruited by other universities around the country. I asked his name. I asked it again. I said, "Naw, it couldn't be," but it was! That big bird, the football player, the one whose parents could have done a better job. He had his Ph. D., was a nationally renowned scientist, and served in a stake presidency. Oh yes, he was there with his wife and family. I threw my arms around him and he hugged me so hard it about broke my back. Gratefully, some things never change!

What a joyous reunion we had! It was a grand celebration. We celebrated Aaronic Priesthood boys becoming Melchizedek Priesthood men. We celebrated a bishop who never gave up. We celebrated parents who really had taught correct principles. We celebrated Leo, who had driven all night from California and parked his eighteen-wheeler the full length of our residential lot. I don't know how they did it. I didn't help them. But that Saturday as I sat on the stand in the tabernacle looking out, there they all were seated on the front row. What a special sight! Who could have imagined that that group of boys would one day all be seated together on the front row of the tabernacle for a general priesthood meeting. That weekend we laughed together, we embraced, we cried, we hugged, we talked, we ate together, and prayed together.

The morning after they left we awoke still basking in the glow of such a sweet experience. We walked out on our front porch and there on our little new trees that could hardly hold leaves, we saw that each had been delicately and lovingly adorned with one carefully placed strand of white toilet paper.

As I look back from this vantage point, I realize that twenty years ago I was operating on faith and hope. I had no idea how those teenage boys would turn out. We just all hung in there and hoped for the best. In the ensuing years as I've contemplated that experience, and after adding many more similar experiences to it, I've become convinced that there are a set of important Aaronic Priesthood leadership principles under which Aaronic Priesthood leaders can operate.

I appreciate greatly the opportunity to have served for

five years in the Young Men's General Presidency under the
direction of Elder Jack H. Goaslind, who served as president. During those years we asked ourselves often as a presidency and a board, What would we like to see happen in
the lives of young men of the Church? The discussions led
to a formulation of the mission and objectives of the Aaronic
Priesthood and to a discussion of principles we felt would
be helpful to Aaronic Priesthood leaders. From my experience and those discussions have come six principles that I
think can be helpful. I share them in the hope that their application may bless the lives of young men in the Church.

Principle Number One

Principle number one is that the bishop is president of
the Aaronic Priesthood. This is a clear reaffirmation of the
role of the bishop. The responsibility for teaching gospel
and priesthood principles on Sunday and illustrating them
with practical application during the week rests squarely
with the bishop and his counselors. The bishop may call a
Young Men's presidency and advisors to assist in the work,
but his is a direct mandate to be the "leader" of the Aaronic
Priesthood young men and young women. This mandate is
spelled out clearly in the Doctrine and Covenants. In Section 107:13–15 we read:

> The second priesthood is called the Priesthood of
> Aaron because it was conferred upon Aaron and his
> seed, throughout all their generations.
>
> Why it is called the lesser priesthood is because it is
> an appendage to the greater, or the Melchizedek Priest-
> hood, and has power in administering outward ordi-
> nances.
>
> The bishopric is the presidency of this priesthood,
> and holds the keys or authority of the same.

Verse 15 makes it clear that Aaronic Priesthood leadership must come from the bishop and his counselors.

The calling of bishop is perhaps the most difficult and challenging assignment in the Church. The bishop is the nexus of all that goes on in the ward and has an almost overwhelming number of responsibilities spelled out in the Melchizedek Priesthood Leaders Handbook. Critical to the success of a bishop is the ability to set priorities and manage his time accordingly. To that point it was interesting to have the opportunity over a five-year period, to visit with many bishops about how they spent their time. As a result of those visits, we as a Young Men's presidency observed a wonderful and seemingly curious outcome. We observed that when a bishop gives more time and attention to his Aaronic Priesthood leadership role, indeed when a bishop makes the youth in the ward his number one priority, everything else in the ward seems to go better too.

It is not clear why this would be the case. Several possibilities present themselves. One possibility is that although Melchizedek Priesthood leaders are counseled to completely fulfill their responsibilities and thus relieve the workload of the bishop, it is often difficult for bishops to "let go" of those matters that Melchizedek Priesthood leaders are capable of handling. Thus if a bishop makes the commitment to spend a majority of time with the youth, Melchizedek Priesthood leaders are free to function as they should. Indeed a bishop may encourage Melchizedek Priesthood leaders in their larger roles by spending enough time with the youth that a vacuum is created that draws Melchizedek Priesthood leaders into action.

There is a second possibility, one that I lean to as a father of boys. It is the implicit quid pro quo agreement that is present in the mind of the mother and father of a teenage son. It goes like this: "Bishop, if you're willing to spend time with and advise and counsel and encourage this knuckle-head son . . . You need more temple work done? You need better home teaching? You need us to take charge of the ward social? Bishop, you've got a deal!"

A third possibility is that the Lord is serious about bishops presiding over the Aaronic Priesthood and that when that responsibility is placed front and center the bishop is blessed to be successful.

Whatever the mechanism, bishops who make the youth their number one priority seem to have vibrant, faithful congregations.

Elder Goaslind described an experience he had as a young bishop. Elder Spencer W. Kimball, who was then a member of the Quorum of the Twelve, had come to speak in his ward sacrament meeting. After the meeting, Bishop Goaslind and Elder Kimball were walking down the hall and came upon two young deacons, who were now introduced to the Apostle. As they walked away, Elder Kimball said, "Bishop, you keep your vision down and every adult will look up to you." As the Apostle was getting in his car to leave, Bishop Goaslind asked for clarification. He was told that keeping his vision down meant spending his time with and concentrating on the youth. If he would do that the parents would be coming to him to see what they could do to help, instead of vice versa.

I am convinced that this counsel related by Elder Goaslind is true. Bishops who spend the majority of their time with the youth will have successful youth and success in the rest of the ward as well.

An example might be useful. Not long ago in a training meeting I was discussing the idea that if a bishop would concentrate his time and energy on the youth, everything else in the ward would go better. Several leaders volunteered that they believed very much in that principle and offered their own examples. I share with you a note written by one of those leaders who was serving as a stake president and had previously served not once but twice as a bishop.

When I was called to be bishop the second time, I was determined that the first priority would be the youth—no matter what else happened. When we went into office, there was not a single missionary out, but in the six years we served, every young man who turned mission age completed an honorable mission, without exception. All but two completed their Eagle Scout rank, and all but two of the youth's marriages, both male and female, were in the temple. Due to the great number of missionary meetings (62), our average sacrament meeting attendance for the last three years of our service was 96 percent. The following are some of the things we did:

1. Under no circumstances was a youth interview missed. If they didn't show up, the executive secretary would go pick them up and deliver them.
2. At the twelve-year birthday interview, we would
   a. Set the date for the missionary farewell.
   b. Determine with the parents the amount of money that would need to be deposited each month to acquire enough to finance the mission.
   c. Receive a promise that if a mistake were made that needed to be talked over with the bishop, the young man would call me before sleeping on it a single night, no matter how late it was. Almost always I would get dressed and go to where he was and talk to him that night and give him a priesthood blessing.

3. I would challenge them to read one page of scripture each day and two pages per day the last two months before turning nineteen. This way they could have *all* of the standard works completed by age nineteen.
4. At age eighteen I would begin interviewing monthly that last year before the mission, instead of semi-annually.

This is an example of a bishop who took seriously his role as the president of the Aaronic Priesthood. He taught his quorum members the plan of redemption with enough power and practical application to have an enormous impact on their lives and, by extension, on the whole ward.

In addition to illustrating the principle that a bishop's priority is to be the president of the Aaronic Priesthood, the letter spells out a successful approach for the preparation of missionaries. Notice that among other things, the bishop set a clear expectation by looking into the boy's future and picking a date on the calendar seven years hence. While not mentioned in the letter, I've often suggested that the calendar date could be accompanied by placing the twelve-year-old boy's name on a missionary application and putting it in a folder in the bishop's file drawer. That folder, the application, and the calendar date could be reviewed at each bishop's interview. Incidentally, as I have discussed this letter with priesthood leaders, it has not gone unnoticed by them that the 96 percent attendance at sacrament meeting had a very beneficial effect on the ward budget.

Principle Number Two

Principle number two has to do with helping each young man understand the purposes of the Aaronic Priesthood. It is a tried and true principle that placing a clear set of expectations before an individual is a great key to motivation and achievement. That is part of a leader's job—to help others gain a clear vision of who they are and what they may become.

There are a number of ways this can be done. Let me describe one of them: In May of 1992 I was assigned to speak in the priesthood restoration fireside about some aspect of the Aaronic Priesthood. I wanted eagerly to find some way to capture the imagination of leaders and boys alike relative to Aaronic Priesthood purposes. At that time three of our boys were ages thirteen, fifteen, and seventeen, so I had a deacon, a teacher, and a priest right under my microscope. One evening I was sitting on the edge of the bed talking to one of the boys. During our conversation I looked around the room and suddenly recognized a real possibility.

In that Priesthood Commemoration talk and in many subsequent stake leadership meetings, I have asked the question. "When you go into a boy's room, what do you see on the wall of that room?" The answer is quickly given: Posters! Of whom? Athletes—basketball players, baseball players, football players, soccer players—and sometimes cars and rock bands. I then ask the question. "Why do I ask you (priesthood leaders) what you find on the boy's walls?" The answer always comes back—"Because you want to know who their heroes are, and what they are thinking about." And I reply, "Yes, that's one reason, but why else?" At that point there are a number of responses, but someone usually replies, "Because you want to know if we've been in boy's rooms!" And I say, "voila!"

In my talk I went on to observe how wonderful it would be if every Aaronic Priesthood age boy in the Church had on his wall a poster that listed the six purposes of the Aaronic Priesthood (see Figure 14). Wouldn't it be great if we could move Michael Jordan a little to one side and U2 a little to the other side and right there in a prominent position place a constant visual reminder of who this young man is and what he could and should become?

Figure 14

The Purpose of the Aaronic Priesthood

The purpose of the Aaronic Priesthood is to help each young man—

- Become converted to the gospel of Jesus Christ and live by its teachings.
- Magnify priesthood callings.
- Give meaningful service.
- Prepare to receive the Melchizedek Priesthood.
- Commit to, worthily prepare for, and serve an honorable full-time mission.
- Live worthy to receive temple covenants and prepare to become a worthy husband and father.

Since that talk was given a wonderful thing has happened, and it shows the usefulness of one good idea. From all over the Church, leaders have been thoughtful enough to send copies of their local version of the idea. They come in all shapes, sizes, and colors—some with temples, some with profiles of young men, some with a plaque for the actual picture of the young man to whom the poster is to be given.

As graphic as it is to see in the mind's eye a poster on every wall of every boy, it is only half of the vision. The other half is to envision a knock on the boy's door—it opens, and there stands the bishop, the leader who along with the boy's father epitomizes the values of the Aaronic Priesthood—who is a Melchizedek Priesthood holder, temple endowed, temple married, a loving, serving embodiment of the purposes of the Aaronic Priesthood. He asks to come in, and having made prior arrangements with the mother (this is a step to be overlooked at the priesthood leader's peril), enters the boy's room where the bishop and the boy sit together on the bed. The bishop reviews with the boy each of the six Aaronic Priesthood purposes that are on the poster or plaque in his hand. He paints a vivid picture of who the young man is and who he can become. Together they find a place on the wall where the plaque or poster can be displayed. The poster or plaque, prominently displayed, provides a daily reminder and is a powerful notion. But even more powerful and portable to any place the boy happens to be is the image indelibly engraved on the boy's mind of the bishop sitting with him in his space telling him who he can become, what confidence he has in him and how he stands ready to help the boy achieve that vision. Parents and Aaronic Priesthood leaders owe it to boys to give them a clear set of expectations and a vision.

The value of a personal visit with a visible reminder left behind was clearly demonstrated to me one day in Panama City, Florida. The stake president and I were visiting in members' homes prior to a stake conference. We stopped at the home of a single sister who had joined the Church only six months previously. We were warmly greeted at the door, welcomed into the front room, and introduced to her fourteen-year-old son. After the introduction and without saying another word, this enthusiastic new convert and mother literally ran down the hall to her son's room and quickly returned with a wall plaque in her hand. She related excitedly how a few days earlier the bishop had come to their home and sat on the couch with her and her son and had talked about the Aaronic Priesthood purposes that were on the plaque. They had then walked together down the hall and placed the plaque on the wall. We were told with gratitude of the impact this experience had had on her son as well as on her as a parent.

Principle Number Three:
Teach Doctrine and Principles

The reader will recognize this as a reiteration of the concepts discussed at length in chapter 1. I believe it is important that this principle be emphasized separately in a discussion of leadership principles for Aaronic Priesthood young men and for young women. The issue is the need to state explicitly for this age group the importance of having their behavior begin to be principle based. For emphasis I repeat Elder Packer's quote: "The study of the doctrines of the gospel will improve behavior quicker than a study of behavior will improve behavior."

This concept is illustrated in a subtle but effective way in the study of Latter-day Saint young men done by the Church evaluation division and presented to the Young Men General Board some years ago. The study analyzed the behavior of young men of the Church—their attendance at meetings, their participation in priesthood assignments, their relationship with advisors, and so on. The results of the study were quite revealing. It was concluded that the single most important factor in determining whether or not a young man holds the Melchizedek Priesthood later on in his life is his private religious observance. It's not his attendance at meetings, it's not his participation in the super activity or stake athletic program. Those things are important, but the number one predictor is private religious observance, or in other words understanding of doctrine and principles. Private religious observance is what goes on in the home—personal prayer, family prayer, scripture reading, tithe paying, Sabbath observance. The best predictor of whether or not a young man will really catch the vision of himself as a Melchizedek Priesthood holder, missionary, and husband is his private religious behavior.

That is why teaching doctrine is so important. In Alma 12:32 we read, "Therefore God gave unto them commandments, after having made known unto them the plan of redemption." This verse is not remarkable on the surface. I had read it several times, but one day Elder Boyd K. Packer added an important insight. The issue is the sequence of events; *before* God gave commandments—the do's and don'ts—to his children, He wanted to make sure that they understood the plan. "God gave unto them commandments *after* having made known unto them the plan of redemption." Instructions on what to do, what not to do—commandments, if you will—would be set in context of a plan, a vision.

Visualize again the flow chart on page 14. On the right-hand side is application or behavior. On the far left is doctrine. In the middle are principles. Those of us who are parents or who teach from the pulpit or in any setting, whether priesthood, Relief Society, or family, may spend too much time harping to our youth about behavior, pointing out that they are not doing this right, and how they need to do that better. Our challenge, I believe, is to redress the balance and spend equal time talking to young people about the doctrine and the principles that flow from the doctrine. Doctrine is the foundation. From the doctrine flow certain principles, and from those principles flow certain behaviors which are the application of those principles.

Let me give you an example. Probably the most difficult challenge for young people today is morality. Never before have our youngsters been so bombarded with misinformation and temptation relative to standards of moral behavior. As parents and youth leaders we ought to provide clear, specific conduct guidelines. We need to spend considerable time saying to them: "Don't touch each other in inappropriate places"; "Don't lie beside or on top of each other on couches"; "Don't be out together late alone"; "Do double date with other couples"; and so on. To counterbalance the media, our focus needs to be very much on behavior. But in addition, I wonder how often we sit down with our youngsters and really talk to them about the doctrine and the principles. We may allude to the fact that immorality is next to murder in terms of its seriousness. But have we ever developed a logic that helps them understand why?

The issue is one of authority. Can we explain the concept of authority and God's authority over life? Do we explain that only God has the authority to take and to give life? He reserves that to himself. That authority can be delegated; we can be authorized; as, for example, Nephi was authorized to slay Laban. Men and women are authorized to take a life if they are protecting their homes, families, and children in times of war.

By the same token, we have no right to start life unless we are given the authorization. The issue is not that sex is wrong or evil. The issue is authority. We don't have the right to start a life, and we don't have the right to take a life unless and until we are given that authority. If we explain the doctrine to our young people, then we can lay out some logical principles regarding our commitment to chastity and applications of those principles. Whenever we teach our youngsters, we would make more progress by first backing up a step or two to make sure that the doctrine is understood.

Often leaders want us to give specific and detailed prescriptions for every possible situation. For instance, several years ago a young women leader called to ask if the Church would specify a policy about fourteen-year-old girls attending afternoon dances. We talked at length and I tried to help her see that in a Church of ten million members in nearly 150 countries it is not practical or possible to provide a paragraph description of every possible application. It might be nice to be able to point to a rule from the prophet for every possible situation, but that's not the principle of agency. We want to avoid the IRS problem alluded to in chapter 1. The Church explains tithing with a ten-word description: give 10 percent of your increase on an annual basis. The IRS has shelves and shelves full of code books attempting to detail every specific kind of income and each exact kind of tax that ought to be paid, specifying all possible expenses and deductions, and so on and so forth. As leaders and parents, instead of turning to a code book, let's talk with our youth about doctrine and help them identify principles that flow from doctrine. Then let's talk with them about reasonable applications.

This is a process we should engage in ourselves as we solve problems at a local level. Should a fourteen-year-old girl attend a matinee dance? What makes sense? Local parents and leaders can identify the principles that are relevant and then discuss together with the youth the application issues involving time, place, manner, and so on. The result should be a matinee dance policy that is in keeping with general principles and also right for local circumstances. Talking about the applications, and helping young people understand the whys, becomes the basis for them to develop independence and the ability to cope with the tremendous number of influences from the world around them. These influences only become more complex and complicated as they grow older. If we can ground the young people strongly in doctrines and principles, they can figure out the applications.

Principle Number Four

The fourth principle of the Aaronic Priesthood is, "Boys need wood to chop." The principle is that for leaders to be successful with young men they (the young men) need to be involved in meaningful priesthood work. Someone observed that the youth need to see themselves as part of the engine and not part of the baggage. The same idea is embodied in the statement that the pioneers would never have made it across the plains if the teenagers had ridden in the wagons. It has become an increasing challenge in modern industrialized society to involve young people in the meaningful efforts of the family and society. We relegate them to a position of being "entertained." This is not so much a conscious decision, but it occurs by default in our more complex society.

Anyone who has worked with youth knows that when they see themselves as important to the achievement of something they understand and believe in, the results can be wonderful indeed. Let me illustrate with an example.

Some years ago a long-time friend visited our home and I found he had been serving for several years as a bishop. I asked how his ward was doing. He said "Fine." Now, I had known this man for twenty years and knew him to be an outstanding leader, so probed a little more. I asked about his sacrament meeting attendance, temple activity, and home teaching—how did he think things were going. Again he said "Fine."

So I got more pointed. I said, "Bishop, tell me, would you say your ward leads the stake in most measures?" He allowed as how it probably did. Now I was able to get where I wanted to go. "What is it," I asked, "that makes your ward so successful?" He modestly replied, "Well, we have really good people." I encouraged him to be more specific. After thinking for a minute he said, "I believe the reason our ward works so well is that I spend 80 percent of my time with the youth."

I said to myself, "Ahh! Principle number one!"

He then gave a wonderful illustration of the wood-to-chop concept. He explained that the bishopric had some months ago received a request to provide a list of names of adults in the ward who knew something about computers and who might be able to do name extraction work. After going down the ward roster, they had compiled a list of fifteen or so adults who they had reason to believe knew something about computers. As they looked at the list, one of the counselors observed that every teenager in the ward knew more about computers than any adult on the list. They all laughed, but an idea was sown.

So the bishop went to some of the priests and laurels in the ward—told them they had a computer-related project they needed help with, and asked if they would mind helping out. They quickly learned the routine, involved themselves eagerly, and after a few weeks they came with a question. "Bishop, what happens with all these names?" So the good bishop put on his hat labeled "Teacher of the Plan of Redemption" and taught them about performing ordinances for the dead and explained that in those names there could be the very name they could be baptized for in the temple. They said, "Well, then bishop, we have a problem. We can't possibly do all these names in the two temple trips we have planned for this year." "So what do you suggest?" asked the bishop. "Well, bishop, it's obvious we just have to go more often." They went eight times.

On one of those trips, someone raised another question: "Bishop, what happens to these names after the temple baptism is done for them?" So the bishop again put on his special hat, ready now to teach the doctrine. In sensitive and appropriate ways, he taught them about the temple endowment and sealing ordinances. They asked, "Bishop, who's in charge of making sure that work is done?" The bishop said, "Well, your parents are, I guess." When they asked, "Bishop, how are they doing?" The bishop hedged—"Well . . . well . . ." So they said, "Now look, bishop, we can't let these people sit in some dead letter file here. We've got to figure out how to get this work done! What can we do to help you get our parents to the temple? Can we babysit? What can we do?"

Do you see the power of getting these youngsters involved in being part of the engine and not part of the baggage? When you do that, all of a sudden they begin to pull the whole load forward. The bishop went on to explain that his attention to the youth and their involvement in meaningful priesthood work provided the spark that ignited the whole ward. That ward had the highest temple attendance in the stake, the most temple baptisms for the dead, and the highest sacrament meeting attendance, because young men and women were a working part of that wonderful engine.

Principle Number Five:
The Role of the Quorum Presidency

It was Sunday morning at our home. I was worrying about something or other that I'm sure I thought was important, and I only vaguely remembered that the twins had mentioned someone was coming to see them and could Margaret and I be present. The doorbell rang, and after a minute or two I was summoned to the front room. I greeted our visitors and then sat down still engrossed in my own thoughts.

After a few minutes I began to focus on what was happening. There in our front room were four twelve- and thirteen-year-old young men dressed in white shirts and ties along with two adult men similarly attired. As I sat and absorbed the scene, I realized that something very interesting was happening. I was listening for adult voices and not hearing any! The men were not talking, Margaret and I were not talking. In fact, all the talking was being done by the boys!

The boys in our front room constituted the deacons quorum presidency for our ward. Our twins had turned twelve, and the presidency had come to welcome them into the quorum and give them instructions about passing the sacrament, collecting fast offerings, and what to plan on for activity night. It was very impressive. It was obvious that there had been significant time spent by adult advisors in the preparation and training of these young men to function as a presidency. But what a wonderful blessing—to learn about presiding, about delegation and follow-through, about how to welcome new members into the quorum. And what a blessing to the boys being welcomed—to know that their peers were excited about their being part of the group!

Principle number five in Aaronic Priesthood leadership is to recognize the role of the quorum presidency. It is clear that the bishopric is the presidency of the Aaronic Priesthood, but it is very important that the deacons quorum presidency, teachers quorum presidency, and assistants to the bishop for the priests quorum be taught and allowed to function in their leadership responsibilities. It certainly requires more patience, time, and skill for advisors to teach the boys how to do something than it would take to do it themselves. Whoever made the statement that one boy is worth a man, two boys is half a man, and three boys is no man at all probably spent time as a deacons quorum advisor. But even small successes in leadership training can have major impacts. That wonderful priests quorum reunion spoken of earlier reminded me that we're building for the future.

In several instances when stake presidents have commented on the weakness of elders quorum leadership I've wondered what an impact could be had if Aaronic Priesthood holders were trained to preside over a quorum. In such cases, ten years later there would be fewer inactive elders and those that were active would be better leaders.

Principle Number Six:
A Cadre of Caring Adults

I sometimes mention an unconfirmed statistic that 90 percent of young men who become Eagle Scouts also serve missions. The natural reaction to this is to ask, What is it about being an Eagle Scout that relates to missionary service? Is it camping, cooking, and hiking? Is it perseverance in rank advancement? Is it learning to take responsibility, be a leader, follow through?

Each of these factors may play a part, but it is interesting to note that a high correlation between Eagle Scout achievement and mission service does not necessarily imply causation. In other words, the fact that the two are somehow strongly related does not mean that one is caused by the other. It may in fact be the case that becoming both an Eagle Scout and a missionary is related to some other factor.

It is my belief that the critical factor is the existence in the boy's life of a strong cadre of caring adults made up of parents and ward youth leaders.

I believe there is a special genius in the Scout program for achieving the Aaronic Priesthood mission of seeing young men become Melchizedek Priesthood holders, serve missions, marry in the temple, and become leaders in the Church. That genius is not direct or even visible to the casual observer. The genius is that the program is a vehicle for enlisting, organizing, and developing an infrastructure of caring adults. It is that infrastructure that helps a boy become an Eagle Scout and when kept in place is a critical part of helping him become a missionary.

Wards have successful Scouting programs when the bishopric makes Scouting a priority and where all the assistant Scoutmaster, assistant Explorer advisor, advancement chairmen, committee chairmen, transportation committee, and so on, positions are filled and functioning. The primary objective would appear to be to provide Scouting activities and advancement for boys. What really happens in a successful Scouting program, one that produces Eagle Scouts, is that mothers are involved, fathers are involved, many men in the ward are involved, and the combined cadre of adults helps produce an Eagle Scout. When that wonderful, committed infrastructure is in place is it any wonder that Eagle Scouts become missionaries!

When ward leaders are lukewarm toward Scouting or approach it half-heartedly, it is predictable that fewer boys will achieve the rank of Eagle. It is more than likely that in some cases the same half-hearted effort will result in a degenerate (flimsy) infrastructure, and the result will be many fewer missionaries serving than would otherwise be the case.

It must be clearly stated that the mission or purpose of the Aaronic Priesthood should be the focus of the Aaronic Priesthood program. Scouting must not be the tail that wags the priesthood dog. Some Aaronic Priesthood leaders have expressed concerns that that may have become the case. Scouting as an activity program for boys must be subordinate to and consistent with the Aaronic Priesthood purposes. While challenges to the traditional program of Boy Scouts of America from homosexuals and atheists may force the Church to reconsider its commitment to the Scouting program, to date that has not happened. If and when it ever did, we would have inspired counsel from a prophet to guide our next steps. In the meantime, I can say that while in the Young Men Presidency we gave serious consideration to the Scouting program in all its ramifications—budgets, Scout camps, cost of awards, impact on Young Women, and so on—it was our opinion then (1996) and remains my opinion today, that the Scouting program is unquestionably the best thing we can presently be doing for our young men.

The *Deseret News* edition of September 10, 1997, reported on the National Longitudinal Study on Adolescent Health, a survey of roughly 90,000 teenagers. The paper reported: "The primacy of peer relationships has been a widely held concept among professionals since the 1960s. 'There's been a pretty significant myth that peer groups are important and parents are not,' Blum said. [Dr. Robert Blum is one of the study's researchers and the director of the Adolescent Health Program at the University of Minnesota.] 'We've focused so tremendously on peer pressure and instituted so many things to deal with peer pressure. And what this study is saying is that family involvement matters. . . . We invest heavily in role development but that's not where the action is. The action is in *adults connecting with kids!*'"

Modern-day prophets have repeatedly stressed the importance of the family. It is reminiscent of our experience with the Word of Wisdom. Modern medical research has resoundingly upheld the soundness of the health principles outlined in the revelation. In like manner, social science research will undoubtedly do the same for the Church's emphasis on families.

The focus of our activity programs for both young men and young women should be on providing opportunities for adults to "connect with kids." Weekday activities, summer camps, youth conferences, firesides, and so forth, are tried and true vehicles for promoting interaction. As observed earlier, the genius of the Scout program is to "institutionalize" the connecting by having many men fill positions that require interaction with young men.

From my own experience I can offer an example of how this works. As a Scoutmaster years ago, I was having trouble getting the boys through the required merit badges. It seemed that boys were entering the troop just after we had worked on a merit badge they needed and we could never get them caught up. Additionally it was difficult to administer a weekday activity program, periodic camping experiences, and summer camps, and maintain a systematic advancement program. Mostly out of self-preservation, we hit upon an idea that really made a difference. We asked the bishopric to call an adult to be in charge of helping the boys achieve one of the required merit badges each month.

For example, Sister Smith was responsible for helping each boy (of whatever age—Scout, Varsity, or Explorer) obtain the citizenship in the nation merit badge during the month of February. Brother Jones was in charge of safety in the month of March. And so on. In this way, no matter when during the year a boy entered the troop, by the time he had been in the troop a year he would have completed all the required merit badges. We had eleven required merit badges (now there are twelve), eleven months, and eleven different adults—both men and women who were committed to help for their assigned month. The process was repeated each year, so every February Sister Smith taught citizenship in the nation to boys who had entered the troop, moved into the ward, or missed getting that particular merit badge for whatever reason.

And though the program was initiated mostly for my sanity, I noticed an interesting thing. Sister Smith was talking to boys before sacrament meeting. She was attending Eagle Courts of Honor. She was sitting there in missionary farewells and even on occasion inviting several boys to her home for Sunday dinner. She had become part of a cadre of caring adults unwittingly assembled who, once in place, continued to connect with, inspire, support, and motivate boys right through to Melchizedek Priesthood, missionary service, and temple marriage.

For a variety of reasons, the Scouting program does not work in most of the rest of the world as it does in the United States. With that in mind, the First Presidency has authorized a program of weekday activities with recognition for achievement and progress which is designed to support the purposes of the Aaronic Priesthood. That program is being gradually introduced and adopted and the reports of its success are growing. I mention it to give emphasis to the principle. Aaronic Priesthood and Young Women leaders will be successful in helping our youth when part of their effort is directed at building a cadre of caring adults.

I believe that a bishop could gather together all the adults in the ward—youthful adults, middle-aged adults, and senior adults. In such a gathering the bishop could say something like this: "Brothers and Sisters, we have gathered you all together, old and young alike, for a specific purpose. We have wonderful young people in our ward. They have great promise; we love them and we wish to see them realize all their God-like potential. But we need your help. We need to make up our collective minds—all of us together—that we are just not going to let these young people fail. We invite (not challenge) you to be part of our ward cadre of caring adults. We invite you to smile at and call a teenager in our ward by name and inquire about his or her interests. We invite you to attend a choir concert, ball game, or dance recital, and be a visual support. We invite you to invite a young person to dinner, tell them about your job or your hobby or your glory days as a high school athlete. We invite you to hire them to work in your yard or in your house and talk to them while they do it. You grandmothers and grandfathers have wisdom and love to share. You young marrieds have enthusiasm and vitality to share. We want to try this for three months and see what happens. We hope you could do just one thing a week—one interaction in the hall at church, one visit in the neighborhood, one invitation to dinner. Together we can make a huge difference. Won't you please accept this invitation to be part of our ward cadre of caring adults?"

I believe that, given such an invitation, the adults would

respond with an outpouring of interest, love, and concern that would reach out and enfold the youth, who would feel it and respond to it. And all our lives would be blessed. The genius in a successful program for youth is in the connecting of youth with caring adults and in the building of an infrastructure that will stay in place to love, support, strengthen, and never give up till our youth are successful adults.

In summary, there are six principles for Aaronic Priesthood leadership, which when prayerfully applied, have enormous power to bless lives, change hearts, and prepare young men to be noble Melchizedek Priesthood holders. The principles are:

1. The bishop is the president of the Aaronic Priesthood.

2. Teach the mission and the purposes of the Aaronic Priesthood.

3. Teach doctrine and principles.

4. Provide young men with meaningful priesthood work (boys need wood to chop).

5. Honor the quorum president's role and teach the presidency leadership principles.

6. Enlist a cadre of caring adults.

Checklist for Aaronic Priesthood Leaders

1.____ Are the Aaronic Priesthood young men actively led by the ward bishopric or branch presidency?

2.____ Is the bishop or branch president personally involved in teaching the plan of redemption?

3.____ Do the young men have a clear vision of who they are and who they can become?

4.____ Do the young men have meaningful priesthood work to do?

5.____ Are the Young Men presidency members trained in their duties and responsibilities?

6.____ Does the ward or branch have a cadre of caring adults who are determined to help the young men succeed?

CHAPTER FIVE

LEADERSHIP PROCESS

There is a time-tested adage about communication that in the vernacular says: "Tell 'em what you're gonna tell 'em, then tell 'em, then tell 'em what ya told 'em." Let me tell you what I hope I've said.

The Church is growing rapidly in a very complex environment and must have effective priesthood leadership. Leadership is different than management. The biggest challenge for today's priesthood leaders is to do a few right things. I believe there are three *right* things that, if done prayerfully and diligently, will make priesthood leaders powerful and effective in moving forward the Lord's work. They are:

I. Teach the Plan of Redemption

This is number one for three reasons. First, from a spiritual perspective, we learn from Alma 13 that it is the ordained responsibility of every Melchizedek Priesthood holder to be a teacher of the plan of redemption. Second, we know secularly that leaders are those who epitomize the values of the group. Third, as a practical matter, talking about doctrine and principles does more to change behavior than does talking about behavior.

II. Minister

Ministering, serving, and blessing lives is an essential aspect of the gospel and of priesthood leadership. Because charity is the essence of Christian behavior, its understanding and guileless practice must be present in those who lead. When members realize that the leader genuinely loves and cares about them they are more willing to be led.

III. Have Vision and Focus

Only by developing, articulating, and sharing a clear, achievable picture of the future can the priesthood leader begin to effectively move the work forward. That view of what can be achieved by the quorum, ward, or stake must be consistent with the mission of the Church and with direction from the presiding authority. The organizational vision must be focused into two or three, at the most, carefully targeted, well-defined and measurable objectives. Objectives are chosen that have maximum collateral value and thereby, when accomplished, have had a major impact on the whole organization.

These are the three essential activities that define leadership, separate leaders from managers, and make it possible to be effective. In summary, the three Roman numeral ideas and questions leaders should ask themselves are reproduced as Figure 15. I have chosen to spend a chapter on each of these three essential concepts of priesthood leadership. I believe they can be understood and applied by priesthood holders throughout the Church in any country and at any level of priesthood responsibility. For the

Figure 15

Effective Priesthood Leaders

I. Teach the Plan of Redemption

- Do I take time to study and understand the principles of the plan of redemption so I can teach them clearly?
- Do I teach the plan to my family members, to my quorum, ward, or stake members, and to my friends and neighbors?
- Do I teach the plan in sacrament meeting, leadership meetings, ward and stake conferences, in interviews and counseling opportunities?

II. Minister

- Is my ministering personal in nature or only a response to institutional assignments?
- If I find it hard to genuinely care about others, what could I do to change?
- Am I trying to follow the example of the Savior?

III. Have Vision and Focus

- Do I understand the mission of the Church?
- What group could help me catch a workable vision of what could be done?
- What two or three things could be focused on?
- How could progress in the focused outcomes be measured?

remainder of this chapter, I want to say something about three other ideas that I believe are important in leadership.

I hope I have made the point that an effective leader must do a few right things. I don't believe six is a "few," so I proceed with trepidation and the hope that adding ideas doesn't dilute my effort to focus leaders on the three essential concepts already discussed.

Having said that, let me introduce this notion: Leadership in any endeavor, including the priesthood, is more effective if attention is paid to something I will label as "process." Consideration must be given for how things are done and how interactions take place between the priesthood leader and members of the stake, ward, or quorum.

As an example, consider the recently widowed woman who approached the bishop and expressed her sadness at never again being able to pray in sacrament meeting. When asked by the bishop why she would think she would never again be asked to pray in sacrament meeting, she explained, "Bishop, I've observed that you always have a husband and wife offer the sacrament meeting prayers, and since my husband is now dead, it seems to me I won't ever have that opportunity again."

After a few moments of thought, the bishop realized that the problem stemmed from a misguided process— when the sacrament meeting program was being organized by a member of the bishopric the practice was to make a telephone call to a member family and request two prayers! One telephone call for two prayers was efficient, but in this case not effective for blessing the lives of ward members.

The process was exclusive not inclusive. It was efficient but not effective. I believe effective leaders learn to manage the processes or the ways an organization goes about doing things. In tending to process, an effective leader addresses the needs that individuals exhibit when they are part of an organization. Have you ever asked yourself the following

questions? Why do I want to be involved in a particular organization; why give time and effort to this organization instead of a variety of others? What are the commitment, pas-
sion, excitement or enthusiasm factors that make me want
to associate and give my best effort? Consider, among others, these six needs or factors.

- To be involved in something with purpose
- To know leaders and others care
- To share in progress and success
- To be part of a team
- To know what's going on
- To have fun

Of course, I believe that people join the Church because
it is true. But are they committed, enthusiastic, excited, and
retained?

Notice, interestingly enough, that the first three needs
or commitment factors have been addressed in Roman
numbers I, II, and III. Teaching the doctrines of salvation
and thereby bringing souls unto Christ speaks dramatically
to factor 1—*being involved in something with purpose.* Our
ministering and serving should send strong signals about
factor 2—*that leaders and others care about members of the organization.* Factor 3—*to share in progress and success*—is realized when leaders have a vision and focus on its accomplishment. The remaining three factors constitute the three
ideas I would like to say something about.

A Team Process

Not too long ago I found myself in an interesting setting. I was with a group of medical doctors in a training session. The doctors had recently assumed management responsibilities and were interested in improving their

leadership and management skills. Some of them had emergency-room work experience and all had had some emergency medical training. They were certainly individuals of significant ability when measured by high science aptitude, grades in school, and graduate training. They had excelled in their medical practices and were viewed by their peers as outstanding doctors and leaders in the medical profession. They acknowledged that they were type "A" personalities and had operated in an environment where a premium was placed on individual decision-making and individual "brilliance." They recognized that they were used to giving orders and being viewed as experts whose decisions and judgment were not often questioned. Nevertheless, they were eager to set aside those self-assessments and learn all they could about leadership.

Into that setting was introduced a trainer and a very interesting leadership-oriented exercise. The exercise exists in a number of variations but each is designed to illustrate the same important principle. The particular exercise that day was called the earthquake game.

In the earthquake exercise participants are asked to assume that an earthquake has trapped them in the basement of a building from which they are not likely to be rescued for at least forty-eight hours. There are a number of items in the basement, such as communications devices, day-old chicken salad sandwiches, matches, water heaters, and so forth. In addition there are bleeding colleagues, gas leaks, and other more and less dire circumstances.

The objective is survival, so each individual playing the game is given a list of fifteen items and asked to prioritize the list from one to fifteen, depending on the individual's assessment of how important the item is to his or her survival.

It is important to note that each participant is given a copy of the exercise and asked to complete it on his own

without conferring with anyone. After each individual com-
pletes the exercise of ranking the items according to their
usefulness, all participants are divided into teams of four to
six persons. The goal of each team is to go back over the exercise and prepare a new team ranking of the items that re-
flects team discussion and analysis. When all teams have
completed their rankings, each person receives a sheet con-
taining the "correct" answers as prepared by a panel of experts.

A score is obtained for each individual by comparing
the experts' answers to those of the individual. A score is
then computed for the team by comparing the team score to
that of the experts.

Now here's the interesting part! In almost every case, the
team score is *higher* than the score for any individual member of the team.

It was fascinating to see the reaction of my doctor
friends who participated in this exercise. When the teams
were made up the trainer invited some of the secretaries
and other onlookers to be part of the exercise and join a
team. As it turned out, several teams had only doctors on
the team while the remaining teams had at least one secretary or other person with a nonmedical background.

Remember that the exercise is an emergency-type exercise. An examination of the items to be ranked reveals that a
number of them have a medical orientation and that someone with medical training would seem to have an advantage
in ranking the items according to their importance. That
was certainly the notion that all the participants had when
they attacked the exercise. Imagine their surprise when it
turned out that the teams that did the best were those that
had team members who were secretaries! Of the all-doctor
teams, the one that did best had a team member who was a
woman. The team that did the worst was the all-male, all-
doctor team!

What an interesting outcome! But it vividly illustrates a very important leadership principle. Leadership in today's complex environment and organizations is often better accomplished by team leaders than by brilliant individualists. There are too many variables, too many inputs, too many possibilities, and too many rapid changes for any one individual acting alone to process and manage.

It was very useful for the doctors participating in the leadership training to realize that teams of non-doctors and non-males had the highest performance. This principle is true in almost all of our endeavors, and it is true in the Church. Effective Church leadership requires a team approach and attention to group processes.

Here I wish to issue a reader *alert!* A team approach and the use of effective group processes are not in conflict with an individual priesthood leader's responsibility to seek the spirit of inspiration and revelation and lead through inspired decision-making. A review of the counsel given to Oliver Cowdery in the Doctrine and Covenants, section 9, is instructive. The setting is the experience that Oliver had early in Joseph Smith's translating of the Book of Mormon when apparently Oliver desired to translate in a manner similar to that of the Prophet Joseph. Oliver was told by the Lord, "Behold, you have not understood; you have supposed that I would give it unto you, when you took no thought save it was to ask me" (D&C 9:7). The Lord was telling Oliver that he could not be inspired out of thin air. The process of inspiration required some thought or effort or analysis on his part. Indeed it is while one is earnestly engaged in the process of seeking information, analyzing it, carefully weighing alternatives, and considering their implementation that inspiration often comes.

The challenge this principle raises for priesthood leaders in the Church today is to recognize the difference between efficiency and effectiveness. It is certainly more efficient for a bishopric or stake presidency to consider an issue and make a decision without seeking input or doing much analysis. There is a class of decisions where confidentiality or other such concerns dictate that decisions be made by the priesthood leader acting alone or at most in counsel with his two counselors. In such cases both efficiency and effectiveness are usually best served by individual as opposed to group action. Even in these situations, wise leaders have learned that gathering all possible information, giving careful thought to alternatives, and performing substantial analysis are prerequisites to receiving inspiration from the Lord.

There are, however, many situations where a priesthood leader can be most effective when he conceives of himself as a team leader. Too many times the scenario seems to go as follows: A ward member approaches the bishop and says, "Bishop, I don't wish to be critical, but our ward seems to have a problem with _____" (the reader can fill in the blank). There are many choices for filling the blank: reverence, missionary work, retention of new converts, reactivation, friendliness or lack thereof, and so on. The bishop says, "Thank you, Brother Brown. We'll take that up in our bishopric meeting and get back to you." The bishop and counselors meet, discuss the matter, and decide to make some assignments. The assignments are made and time passes. Brother Brown inquires, or the stake president inquires, about a matter that was handled similarly, and the bishop replies. "Well, Brother Brown (or President Jones), we met for a long time as a bishopric and made some assignments but—well, you know how things go in the Church."

The problem here is that modern organizations are complex, with many relationships and many facets to a problem. Organization members need to be involved in discussion, analysis, and solution alternatives in order for anything to change. If the priesthood leader wants to see something happen, he has to think of himself as the leader of a team. The appropriate leadership team in the ward is the ward council. In the stake it is the stake council. Now into the reader's mind should come the image of Elder Ballard trying with all his might to get priesthood leaders to understand the importance of councils. The ward or stake council is the leadership team that when appropriately led can do wondrous things.

One of the most egregious priesthood leadership shortcomings in the Church today is lack of skill in involving the broader ward and especially the sisters of the Church in problem identification, analysis, and solution. For the most part, I don't believe it's intentional. I believe it's because many priesthood leaders operate with a military, hierarchical leadership model which suggests that some are above and some are below. Communication goes up the ranks and orders go back down the ranks. That model may work in combat conditions, but research has shown that it does not work well in most modern organizations and certainly is suboptional in the Church. The military model does appear at first blush to be very time-efficient, and no one can fault a priesthood leader who has a forty-hour (at least) a week job and a family for being a fan of efficiency. Furthermore, group processes are messy. The group can get off track, and people with strong opinions and good verbal skills can inappropriately dominate the process. And there is always the legitimate question about how inspiration to an ordained, set-apart leader is integrated with a group process.

And so perhaps it's easy to see why many priesthood leaders operate the way they do. The model is simple and well understood, it's quick, efficient, and tidy. The problem is, it just doesn't work very well! It may be efficient but it is not *effective*. The time that is saved by some at the top is illusory. When the process provides no results, the time is really wasted. It really shouldn't be a surprise when the situation is thoughtfully pondered. When any problem in a ward or stake is considered only by the priesthood, many of the resources for problem identification, analysis, and solution are unavailable to the leader. In extreme cases where ward and stake councils are not used, the result is that one-half the whole ward or stake represented by the sisters is left out of the process. The situation is not much better when all that goes on in a council meeting is the coordination of calendars and the giving out of assignments.

Priesthood leaders, attention! This is *not* fundamentally a male-female problem or a priesthood-sister problem. The same problem would exist if the ward or stake faced a serious challenge with their youth and the youth and their parents were left out of the problem-solving process. The fundamental issue is how priesthood leaders go about the process of leadership. The process must be inclusive. The effective priesthood leader is a team leader. Everyone on the team is a member of the Church and cares about its success. Each should be given equal opportunity for input as well as some opportunity to shoulder responsibility for outcomes. Please note! Team leadership is *not* decision-making by vote or group confusion with no one in charge.

Final decisions must be made by ordained, set-apart priesthood leaders. But the best decisions will be made by those leaders who have allowed the process to provide input and stimulate inspiration.

Inclusive Communication

It's natural for someone in an organization to want to know what's going on. Those feelings can be ignored by leaders or they can be used to strengthen commitment and enthusiasm. The trouble is that communication with group members takes time and effort. To a busy leader it may not seem to be an efficient use of resources. And there is always a legitimate question about what can and should be communicated and what is best handled in a more confidential manner. Every organization struggles with these issues, and the Church is no exception.

Priesthood leaders at all levels are counseled extensively and appropriately about the importance of maintaining confidentiality when dealing with sensitive information concerning members' lives and conduct. This confidentiality is essential to the repentance process and must exist for leaders to maintain the confidence of Church members. This principle cannot be overstated. Having said that, I also believe there are opportunities for legitimate inclusive communication that will be appropriate, welcome, and will strengthen the leadership process. The challenge for priesthood leaders is to identify those issues which need to be communicated openly and then go to the effort to provide that communication.

I observed such a situation in a firsthand manner. Our ward has a new bishop and a large number of Young Women and Aaronic Priesthood holders. The bishop invited all twelve- to eighteen-year-old youth and their parents to attend a Sunday evening bishop's fireside talk in the ward chapel. The bishop spoke plainly to the combined group about the challenges facing youth and about standards found in the Church publication "For the Strength of Youth." I hope this seems unremarkable to the reader and that it is occurring all over the Church as an example of good, inclusive communication. However, the bishop went beyond just calling a meeting and speaking effectively to parents and youth. He explained to those assembled that *before* having the combined meeting he had spent several hours with the Bishop's Youth Committee and had sought their input and counsel on the matters to be discussed and standards to be set. In particular, he had asked them if it was reasonable to adhere to the "no dating before sixteen" guideline. They reassured him that it was, and because he had counseled with them and had included the youth leaders in the communication process he was then able to solicit the support of parents and youth alike in reaffirming that standard for all the youth in the ward.

Other examples of inclusive communication could include 1) a discussion of the ward budget and amounts spent on Aaronic Priesthood and Young Women programs, 2) a discussion of building usage and maintenance, and 3) a discussion of ward or stake boundaries, and meeting schedules.

The principle is straightforward. Inclusive communication speaks to the need that group members have to know what's going on. Of course, leadership can be exerted without paying attention to the process of communicating openly about all appropriate issues. This is especially true in the Church, where the legitimate need for confidentiality in some matters can be misconstrued as reason not to communicate well on any matters. However, effective priesthood leaders will find ways to establish, wherever possible, inclusive rather than exclusive processes. The effort put forth to establish inclusive processes will be returned manyfold in increased commitment and enthusiasm and will provide the leader with leverage to accomplish the mission of the Church.

Esprit de Corps

Esprit de corps is defined in the American Heritage Dictionary as a spirit of devotion and enthusiasm among members of a group for one another, their group, and its purposes. A group that has the spirit accomplishes its purposes, has strong ties with its members, and is fun to be a part of. Wise leaders can promote these feelings in appropriate ways and observe marked improvement in group performance. Most athletic teams exhibit *esprit de corps*. It exists in many successful business, military, and patriotic organizations and is generally recognized as a major factor in their success. But is this principle appropriate for use in the Church? For example, do we as Church leaders want to promote a gung ho, rah, rah attitude about our Church activity and expect a dedication that excludes any other activity or association? Is it appropriate in the Church to think in terms of having fun? (I know a Church leader who says if you're not having fun you're not doing it right. I believe he makes an important point.)

I can remember an interesting example of *esprit de corps* from long-ago years in the mission field. There were two districts of missionaries serving in the city of Bordeaux in southern France. In an attempt to promote some enthusiasm and have fun, a P-day touch football game was proposed. It sounded like a good idea, but there was one reservation: The new district leader of one of the districts hardly seemed the type to participate in a football game. He was refined, polished, articulate, and had an aristocratic bearing and carriage that was very unusual. His French was superb, he was always impeccably dressed, and his delicate and artistic hands were well suited for the violin, which he played beautifully. He admitted to have never played football but said he would come and watch.

P-day arrived, and all but the district leader assembled attired in clothes appropriate for the muddy, wet field. He came with neatly pressed creases in upscale slacks and a freshly ironed button-down-collar sports shirt. It was all he had and the only way he was comfortable dressing. To our initial amazement and subsequent consternation, he agreed to play.

The defining moment came when, in an awkward attempt to block an opposing player, he was hit hard and sent sprawling headlong into an enormous mud puddle. All motion ceased, and there was a moment of tense silence. He looked at his shirt, at his pants, at his hands, and then to our relief, broke out in the biggest, hardest, sustained laugh we had ever heard. We added our laughter to his as we picked him up and brushed off the mud and water.

In that moment was born a spirit of enthusiasm and devotion to one another and to the leader that began to define that group of missionaries. It defined their leader as different but not aloof; he could join in and laugh. He maintained dignity, gained respect, and promoted an *esprit de corps* that pulled the group together in their missionary work.

What about *esprit de corps* in the Church generally? Is it necessary or appropriate for the bishop to play basketball or go water skiing with the priests? Should the stake president play on his ward softball team or play his guitar in the stake road show? Should the elders quorum president host a potluck dinner and game night in his home every six months? Should a ward hold frequent "ward socials"?

The answer is not the same for every group and every leader. Some leaders use personality and their natural interest to promote closeness, enthusiasm, and spirit. Others feel awkward and uneasy in such attempts. While *esprit de corps* may be an important element in a leader's success, it is not necessary that the leader be personally responsible for initiating and promoting it. Others can bring that element to the group. A wise leader will encourage spirit and elan to come from a young, enthusiastic counselor, the chairman of the Activities Committee, or the Young Women presidency. Of course *esprit de corps* and a sense of fun can be abused. A rah rah, gung ho attitude is not the idea. But warmth, humor, and fun, when controlled and appropriately inserted into the context of reverence for the Savior and His work, can be extremely effective in the process of leadership.

Much more could be said about each of these three "additional" ideas. I have grouped them under the general heading of processes because I believe they speak to how leaders go about their responsibility to move the group forward. If a priesthood leader continually asks himself questions such as: Do my stake, ward, or quorum members feel part of what's going on? Are they "on the team"? Do they feel knowledgeable and included? Are they enjoying themselves, their service, and their experience in the Church?— if he asks himself such questions, he is generally aware of process.

The challenge with all these "processes" in leadership is that they require more effort and attention than the solo leadership style. They go to the heart of efficiency versus effectiveness. Getting everyone "on the team" and including each in the process of problem solving is time consuming and unwieldy. Worrying about whether the group has spirit and enthusiasm for the task may seem to be unrelated to getting at something and getting it done. Being inclusive requires so much more time in communication and interaction than being exclusive. Generating *esprit de corps* and sociability at the appropriate level requires planning and coordinating. None of these processes are quick and easy, but it turns out that they are enormously effective. They can make the difference between being a caretaker and a leader and whether the organization stands still or moves ahead. The bottom line is that these inclusive processes are extraordinarily powerful in generating commitment and resolve to do what is being asked by the leaders.

In conclusion, I'm convinced that a priesthood leader can be effective by doing a few *right* things. A fundamental irreducible foundation must be personal righteousness and the willingness to seek the Spirit and be taught by it. With that foundation in place, the right things are 1) teach the plan of redemption, 2) minister as the Savior would,

3) have vision, and focus that vision on a small number of objectives. If in addition the leader pays attention to the processes necessary to involve members and gain their commitment, he will be a wonderfully effective leader. The leader will be happy and successful, members' lives will be blessed, and the Lord's work will move forward with direction and power.

Priesthood Leader Checklist

— Do I understand the concept of organizational processes?

— Do people I lead consider themselves as part of a team?

— Am I inclusive or exclusive in my organizational communication?

— Am I able to make Church work fun for all involved, or is it drudgery?

Conclusion

In the introduction I observed that the size, scope, and growth of the Church require that for the work to move forward we must have effective leaders. I stated, and I firmly believe, that priesthood leaders must be men of strong characters who have learned to follow the teachings of the Savior and live lives of personal worthiness. I am convinced that men such as these have the right to be taught by the Spirit and that those spiritual teachings will be the best source of leadership training and advice. I sincerely hope that nothing I have written suggests any other view to the reader. Leaders must continually strengthen themselves spiritually through the time-tested methods of scripture study, pondering, fasting, prayer, and temple worship. I do not advocate the use of any leadership principle or approach that does not recognize the importance of the leader's being led by the Spirit. We generally live far below our spiritual privilege, and our goal as leaders ought to be to close that gap.

At the same time I am convinced that the Spirit struggles to operate through an empty vessel. I believe the principles I have outlined merit careful consideration. I believe they work. I have seen them work. I also know they must be thoughtfully and prayerfully adapted to the nearly infinite number of specific individual situations faced by Church leaders around the world.

But in the end isn't that the thrill and satisfaction of the experience? To know that you are called by God to be engaged in the work of building the kingdom and blessing lives. To realize that these are principles and processes that may be helpful. And then to go forward with faith, courage, and enthusiasm—to teach and minister and apply the principles with energy and spiritual insight.

I believe that in the process God will bless us with wisdom, experience, spiritual growth, and success in our callings. That certainly is my hope and prayer for every priesthood leader.

INDEX